The Executive Résumé Handbook

The
Executive Résumé
Handbook

HAROLD W. DICKHUT

PRENTICE HALL PRESS • NEW YORK

Copyright © 1987 by Harold W. Dickhut
All rights reserved, including the right of reproduction
in whole or in part in any form.

Published by Prentice Hall Press
A Division of Simon & Schuster, Inc.
Gulf + Western Building
One Gulf + Western Plaza
New York, NY   10023

PRENTICE HALL PRESS is a trademark of Simon & Schuster, Inc.

Library of Congress Cataloging-in-Publication Data
Dickhut, Harold W.
   The executive résumé handbook.

   Includes index.
   1. Résumés (Employment) 2. Executives.
3. Professions. 4. Job hunting. I. Title.
HF5383.D469   1987   650.1′4′024658   86-22692
ISBN 0-13-294331-X

Manufactured in the United States of America

10 9 8 7 6 5 4 3 2 1

First Edition

CONTENTS

FOREWORD

Changing jobs is something that happens to all of us. For many reasons, good and bad, we find ourselves out of work or wanting to try our luck elsewhere. We change jobs and sometimes even careers.

A job change is always traumatic, but for men and women in higher-level jobs it can be even more difficult. Most of the time people at this level are quite comfortable, and the thought of starting over is more than they can easily handle.

They need help. They now find themselves on the other side of the desk during an employment interview, and they don't know how to proceed. They have read résumés of other applicants but don't know how to write their own. They are smart people but are unprepared.

Fortunately, there is help to prevent them from wasting time, money, and job opportunities. From the depths of his exhaustive background, Hal Dickhut, former president of the Office Management Association of Chicago, has compiled a job-search program that can work for anyone who reads and follows it.

The starting point is the executive résumé. He discusses it, explains how to prepare one, and shows samples that will assuredly produce results. Further, he takes the reader step-by-step through the entire job-search procedure that he, as president of Management Counselors, Inc., developed and that has proved so successful. He concludes with a personalized marketing plan designed to get you the job you want. You can't miss!

Hal Dickhut is unquestionably a leader in this field. All across the country there are successful business and professional people grateful to him for his unselfish interest in them in their time of need. He has written and lectured on this subject, conducted seminars and classes, and counseled individuals. He himself has changed jobs more than a few times, sometimes by choice and sometimes by necessity.

All of this wonderful background and experience, together with his beautiful philosophy of life, are summarized in this convenient book. Read it thoroughly, follow the instructions carefully, and you will end up with the best job of your life.

—WILBERT E. SCHEER
Author, *Personnel Administration Handbook*
Editor, *Human Resources Update* newsletter

PART
I

**Taking
the
First Step**

1

A Complete Program for Marketing Yourself

The Executive Résumé Handbook is devoted to the preparation and successful use of first-rate résumés for corporate and organization executives, professionals, and middle managers. It provides the knowledge, encouragement, and support that will help you in your job search.

In your search for a new job, do you have any objection to saving time, effort, and money? Will practical, proven guidelines make your search easier? Here is a step-by-step "how to" handbook for the individual seeking any top-level position, regardless of earnings, work experience, or age. It lets you control your decisions and marshal your efforts for effectiveness.

The truth about a job search, a career move, or a career change is this: Nobody will or can do it for you. Nobody cares nearly as much as you do. No one can stimulate you or drive you as much as you can. It's really up to you. You can do it best yourself. You've got to work at it as you would at a full-time job and use the tools available to you—a top-notch résumé, a solid job-search plan, and help from others. If you do so, you will succeed.

The Executive Résumé Handbook provides the essentials, the ideas, the stimulation; you provide your background, your achievements, your goals, the decisions required for action. Then you implement some carefully made plans.

Perhaps most important, this handbook will help you overcome your feelings of doubt, indecision, and lethargy and will spur you toward positive action. It is not only a résumé preparation manual, although a fine résumé is imperative. It is also a broadly tested method for marketing yourself.

Finally, this handbook is designed to reinforce your dignity as a human being. It will help to keep you psychologically buoyant as you prepare your effective executive résumé, your job-search campaign, and your program for bringing your efforts to a successful conclusion. So get started—now!

2

Why an Executive Résumé?

WHO NEEDS AN EXECUTIVE RÉSUMÉ?

Do you need an executive résumé if you expect to change jobs? You can be sure you do, because you can't do business without it. You can't convince individuals that they need you and stand to gain if they hire you, and should, therefore, ask you to come see them.

A few people don't need a résumé to get a job, but most do. If you are entering your family's business, or your Uncle Charlie sets you up with his long-time friend, the president of XYZ Corporation, or if you are now the president/CEO of a Fortune 500 company, you may or may not need one. But about 99 percent of us do need résumés in our job searches, and good ones if we are to get the job we want.

Who else needs a superior résumé besides business executives? Professionals do. From the Big Eight to the smallest of accounting firms, a résumé is a foregone requirement for the jobseeker. Do lawyers need résumés? Of course they do. So do college presidents, school district superintendents, high school and grade school principals, and teachers of any grade level. Engineers need résumés. So do doctors, architects, and entertainers. In differing ways, each of these individuals is an executive, either working for someone else or self-employed. Résumés are their word-pictures of themselves.

Who wants a fine, effective résumé? Put yourself in the place of an individual in one of the following three groups and decide if a résumé would help you do your part in the employment procedure.

Potential employers. Business, industry, organizations, the professions, government, and any other classification of employment you can think of demand a résumé.

Executive search consultants/recruiters. These firms will not and cannot work on a search assignment without this tool. There is no way they can consider you, the jobseeker, unless they have an accurate, concise summary of who you are, what you are all about, what your results have been for other employers, and what you want to do for your next employer.

Your contacts. We all tend to assume that our friends and acquaintances know us well. They may know us, but often only within the context of our relationship. Does your tennis partner, professional association committee member, church-member friend, dentist, or civic-leader acquaintance know the details of what you do in your job and what you have achieved? They need to know, and in printed form for reference.

Your résumé forms the basis of what you communicate to others in cover letters, in interviews, and in all other conversations you have about yourself in your job search. Your résumé speaks for you when you aren't present.

The executive résumé is useful not only in getting you interviews. As chapter 4 will discuss, résumé preparation forces you to take a good look at yourself. This sometimes startling self-knowledge can aid you in making career decisions and in getting a job.

Your résumé is a direct on-paper communication to your interviewer, your boss-to-be, and others who may get to vote on hiring you.

THE FINEST POSSIBLE RÉSUMÉ

Your executive résumé is an asset. Well written, it is a tremendous asset. Badly written, it is a liability. And in that case, the negative impression becomes immediately associated with you. So write the best résumé possible!

A superior résumé stacks the odds in your favor. All

those other résumés and letters being considered by the employer have the same purpose as yours: to get the interview. If your résumé is the best, it can make an employer eager to meet you.

Think of how many résumés an employer may get for just one job opening. An interviewer may screen several, or dozens, or hundreds of résumés, depending on the job, the employer, and the market. This is a tough job. The best qualified person doesn't always win the position; the best qualified applicant doesn't always get invited to the interview. Why not? Because all that an interviewer has to go on is a résumé. So a person who is well presented, via a well-written résumé, gets the nod. If you are, in fact, the best candidate for a particular job, all will be lost unless you get the opportunity to sell yourself in person.

No résumé by itself gets you the job. You've heard that advice dozens of times. But an excellent executive résumé will open that important door. On the other side is the person with the power either to refer you upstairs or to hire you. Once inside, the other factors begin to take over: dress and grooming, interviewing ability, body chemistry and interpersonal relations, whether you fit the job, and what you did that brought results to your past employers.

Do you want a 90 percent chance of getting an interview as opposed to a 40 percent chance? Whatever the percentage, a fine résumé puts you ahead of other job-seekers with ordinary résumés. *The Executive Résumé Handbook* shows you how to create an effective and far-better-than-average executive résumé. It's up to you to come up with the best concept and then produce it. Work on your résumé with enthusiasm. It will show up in the final product.

Prepare your personal résumé as if your life depended on it. Actually, your future work-life probably does. You'll feel more confident and more comfortable with a superior word-picture of yourself.

3

Preparing to Change Jobs Now

PRESENT JOB CHECK-CHART

Have you taken a very serious look at your present organization, your present job? You may have already considered the following points. Even if you have, the same factors can be applied to any potential position before you accept an offer.

Job Element	Relative Importance	Current Job Rating	Proposed Job Rating
		(EXCELLENT, GOOD, FAIR, POOR)	
Satisfaction in doing work	1	_____	_____
Freedom to do the job	2	_____	_____
Position in organization	3	_____	_____
Adequacy of earnings	4	_____	_____
Benefits	5	_____	_____
Relationship to management	6	_____	_____
Personal workload	7	_____	_____
Pressure and worry	8	_____	_____

Establish your own order of importance. Add new factors you feel are essential. These might include travel, relocation, extra hours required, or organization atmosphere. Then rate your present work. When you're finished, you will have gotten to know yourself somewhat better.

ANALYZE YOURSELF

Think about your activities and accomplishments in your career and in your personal life. Are you strongest in leadership, research, teaching, organizing? What about selling, mechanical work, persuasiveness, community activity, relating to people, analyzing?

What are you most successful at, not in monetary terms, but in terms of personal satisfaction and achievement? What would you like to do more of?

MOVING UP

Why do you want to climb beyond where you are now? Or even move at all? Perhaps you are tired of your old job, or have, in your judgment, a poor boss. Are you ready? What steps have you taken to prepare yourself? What is your next logical effort? Don't be too quick to say, "That's it. I'm going to get a new job!"

Begin with an honest appraisal of where you stand in your career or organization. What's wrong with your position? Is there any possibility of career advancement with your present employer? Can you afford to discuss it? If so, you had better know what you want to do, where you want to go, and what you can contribute in a new slot. Promotions do not come from employee desire; they are usually based upon previous accomplishments and demonstrated abilities.

BASIC QUESTIONS

Prepare answers to some basic questions about yourself. Be factual and objective.

- Are you outgoing or a loner?
- Do you mix easily in gatherings?
- Can you accept criticism and, more important, make good use of it?
- Do you have a short fuse?

6

- Do you offend quickly?
- Is your judgment respected?
- Can you handle yourself under pressure?
- Do you work best on your own or under supervision, either close or general?
- Are you a confident person?
- Do you regularly use your initiative?
- Are you creative in daily activities?
- Can you delegate effectively?
- Is your self-motivation strong?
- Are your communications clear?
- Are you good at organizing?
- Do you follow through on assignments given to you or that you give?

You can probably think of even more questions about your personal traits and talents. You need to know what you have to sell before you can plan on selling it. Sum up your talents and personal traits before you decide on a job change.

REASONS FOR A JOB CHANGE

Here are some of the primary reasons for changing jobs, divided into two groups. First are those over which you exercise control, where you have a choice of changing or not changing. Second are those over which you have no control.

Your own choice: You vote and decide.

1. To advance your career (the best business reason to change jobs). Your career may be blocked for many reasons; among them, the fact that your employer wants you just where you are, in the best interests of the organization. This may not, however, be in your best interests.
2. To change industries. Maybe you would like to move from an industry that is slipping or already depressed to one that is growth oriented; from a stable, long-established industry just barely holding its own to a high-tech or service-based profession or business. Try to stay ahead and not wait until it's too late. Maybe you are just tired of the industry. Well, why not consider a change?

3. To change organizations or companies. Will a larger or smaller one be better? Are the problems money, the boss, or a desire for a more personal or impersonal work relationship?
4. To improve your position, broaden your experience, or get some needed training. These factors can apply whether you remain where you are or move on.
5. To relocate to a better geographical environment.
6. To enter a new field of work.
7. To earn more to support your family or improve your standard of living.
8. You are worth more in the marketplace, and you know it.
9. You and your immediate superior get along but really don't see eye to eye. You are frustrated, angry, maybe even sick (he or she might be, too).
10. There isn't any fun or satisfaction in your work anymore. Your work-life may be something of a pretense.
11. There is nowhere to go in the organization. Your boss is not much older than you are. (Don't waste the rest of your career!)

Beyond your control: You have no vote. A decisive action has taken place or is about to, or a strong negative condition exists.

1. You have been terminated, for one reason or another. Now the need for a new job is usually urgent and is your chief concern.
2. Your not-for-profit organization loses its funding and can't pay you anymore.
3. A merger has taken place, and your company is now second fiddle.
4. Economic conditions depressed your organization or firm, so you can't be kept on the payroll.
5. Your boss or his or her boss doesn't want you around for some reason.

You need to consider why you want to change jobs now, what your career plan is, who you really are, and why a new employer should want to hire you. If you do this, you will have progressed from seldom thinking deeply about yourself to probing what makes you tick.

4

The First Step in Constructing Your Résumé

Résumé writing begins with data gathering and thinking about yourself. Use the data groups below to help organize your material. Do not expect to use all these headings in your résumé, however. Take an advance look at the sample résumés in chapter 6. Just get the raw facts down on blank paper; if you dig enough you will fill the paper.

This gathering of material shouldn't be mechanical. Now is the time to really think about yourself, all you've done, and how your accomplishments fit into the new job you are seeking. Remember, this material will not only be the basis of your résumé, it will also help you to be accurate and sharp in interviews.

The seventeen areas that follow are all-inclusive for you as a jobseeker. Your work-experience history, responsibilities, and achievements follow as a separate and final part of this section.

Data from the first five areas will normally appear on your résumé. Areas six through nine will often appear, if it is to your advantage. Areas ten through seventeen are listed to alert you to the possibility that one or more may be pertinent to the job you seek. If so, include them. Otherwise, omit these from your résumé. Your individual circumstances will govern which items you include in your résumé. So get started. Read the comments here in the handbook about each item or category. Do all the easy parts first. By the time you start on the most vital area, your work history, you'll be experienced in gathering data.

NAME AND ADDRESS

Use your first name, middle initial, and last name if you normally would in your employment situation. If you usually use initials only, do that. Use a first and last name only, without a middle initial, if that is your practice. Omit nicknames.

Your address is where you expect any correspondence to be sent; it is, in most cases, where you reside. Avoid using a P.O. Box. The phone number you include must be the number at which you can be reached, where a responsible adult will take a business message, or at least, where you can be reached in the evening. Your current office number can be very helpful to a caller; however, you must realize the inherent danger if your present employer is unaware of your efforts to change jobs.

OBJECTIVE

It is essential to state your job objective at the beginning of a résumé. Let's think about those who will read your résumé and how what you say in your job objective statement will affect them.

1. The person who decides whether or not you should be interviewed. He or she may or may not be the one with the final authority to hire.
2. The executive recruiter who seeks an individual who will fit a current search assignment.
3. Your various contacts who can help you get an interview.

Each of these individuals looks at you somewhat differently. Of course, they all eventually need some idea of what you are seeking, but *how* you tell them is key. So before you automatically begin to shape up your phraseology for your objective, consider some reasons why you will want to be very, very careful in doing so.

1. You may limit yourself to what you say. What if the potential employer sees a possibility for you in another area of work? (Be flexible in an interview. See how the wind blows.)
2. If you have two or even three objectives, you might dilute your chances in each area by including them all in one objective. (Solve this by using several résumés.)
3. Your wording may not coincide with what the employer has in mind, even though you actually both seek the same thing.
4. You may overemphasize what you want. Employers are primarily interested in what *they* want.
5. You could irritate your readers with trite phrases, buzz words (e.g., "impact," "challenging," "growth-oriented," "expertise"), or even poor grammar or spelling.

Look at the following job-objective statements that have been taken from actual résumés. Undoubtedly these are all well-intentioned, honest objectives, written primarily by top-level people. Most are too lengthy, however, and state the obvious. Would you use anything similar? Some were copied from other résumés that in turn were copied from other résumés, and so on. Wouldn't the shorter versions be better?

> Career Objective: Challenging Sales/Marketing position with a growth-oriented organization.

Don't we all want a job with a challenge? Doesn't almost every organization think of itself as growth oriented? Since these become empty words, why waste space? Why not say simply "Sales/Marketing"?

> Challenging senior management position as chief financial officer in a growth-oriented company requiring solid financial and accounting management experience.

Any top financial officer needs, and usually has, solid financial and accounting management experience. Now remove the two unnecessary descriptive embellishments discussed above, and what is left? How about "Senior Financial Management"?

> To join a dynamic organization and contribute experience, operations, expertise, and leadership in order to significantly impact company growth and profitability.

This jobseeker fails to say what he or she wants to do. What is more, the writing is bad. You might contribute "to operations" but you can't contribute "operations." The word "impact" when used as a verb means "to force tightly together." You probably wouldn't want to do that to company growth and profitability!

> As an executive with strong drive and the ability to "get things done" quickly and efficiently, I seek a position in the financial community that offers career opportunity, significant responsibility, and immediate challenge. I am particularly qualified as president of a small- to medium-size

financial institution, chief administrative officer, or financial officer.

This could well be a capable, fine executive. But the objective is far too long, has too much descriptive material, and perhaps shows a bit too much ego. The personal pronoun "I" is best omitted from any part of the résumé. This could be shortened to "President/Chief Administrative Officer—Financial Institution."

> Director of public relations/communications (high-technology industry desirable) with opportunity to combine interpersonal, developmental, and organizational skills with a progressive marketing strategy to produce a diverse, effective program.

How's that again? Somehow this writing seems to lack the common touch. It is lengthy. And if sent to any industry other than high-tech, it will be less than effective. (What organization wants to be second choice?) It would be much simpler to say "Director of Public Relations/Communications."

> Associate with a company in the area of sales and marketing where previous experience in medical products and equipment as well as consumer products will contribute to company growth, presenting opportunity for a challenge in management responsibility and mutual long-range advancement.

Since we can't determine the level of this jobseeker, the objective might be condensed to "Sales and Marketing—Medical Products and Equipment/Consumer Products."

Don't hesitate to prepare different résumés or similar résumés with different objectives. Although multiple résumés add up to increased typing and printing costs, they are usually well worth the extra outlay. One pertinent point: In the résumé you send to executive search consultants, an objective should be included, succinctly stated but in terms broad enough so that you do not limit yourself to one position.

In all cases, your objective must be stated somewhere. In addition to your résumé, refer to it in your cover letters, notes, phone calls, and face-to-face conversations. Résumés should never be sent out alone, so a cover letter is an ideal way to say what you are aiming for. There is more on this subject in chapter 10, which is devoted to cover letters.

KNOWLEDGE AND EXPERIENCE SUMMARY

Use concise one-, two-, or three-word phrases that accurately describe your experience/knowledge—not a detailed list of your accomplishments, just what you most certainly know. Not what you should know, but what you do know. Be conservative, for you may be asked to elaborate on one or two items. A weak answer and your interviewer will lose interest. Read through the following examples for various

the lists used in résumés in chapter
list to support your objective. Use
o more.

ADVERTISING

jectives
Campaign Planning
Ad Creation
Direct Mail Campaigns
Media Analysis
Trade Shows

ASSOCIATIONS

Association Management
Trade Association
Industrial Association
Government Relations
Convention Planning
Legislation
Membership Development

BANKING/FINANCE

Senior Administration
Operations Management
Securities Investment
Trust Operations
Business Development
Financial Projections
Long-range Planning
Feasibility Studies

BROKERAGE/SECURITIES

Stocks
Corporate Bonds
Government Securities
Commodity Futures
Money Management
Branch Management
High-volume Selling

COMPUTERS

Methods/Procedures
Software Development
Installations
Applications
Customer Relations

CONSULTING

Corporate Development
Management Surveys
Forecasting
Policy Determination
Executive Training
Manufacturing

CONTROLLERSHIP

Policy Determination
Financial Statements
Profit Planning
Bank Relations
Responsibility Accounting
Expense Control
Computer Installation
Public Accounting
Corporate Secretary

EDUCATION

Staff Supervision
Teaching
School Administration
Proposals/Grants
Curriculum Development
Faculty Relations

ENGINEERING—CHEMICAL

Chemical Engineering
Project Engineering
Materials Testing
New Processes

ENGINEERING—DESIGN

Product Design
Packaging
Tool Design
Shop Scheduling

ENGINEERING—ELECTRICAL

Electrical Engineering
Project Supervision
Computer Control
Hiring/Training

ENGINEERING—ELECTRONICS

Control Electronics
Electro-Mechanical Systems
R & D
New Products
Prototype Fabrication
Production Startup

ENGINEERING—INDUSTRIAL

Production Management
Materials Handling
Distribution Analysis
Facilities Planning

ENGINEERING—MECHANICAL

Production Engineering
Test Equipment
Product Modification
Application Engineering

ENGINEERING—R & D

Forecasts/Budgets
Negotiations/Contracts
Feasibility Studies
Technical Sales
Testing/Evaluation

GENERAL MANAGEMENT

Organizational Structure
Policy Determination
Acquisitions
Trade Relations
Finance
Budgets/Forecasts

LEGAL

Corporate Law
Patent Law
Criminal Law
Real Estate
Trusts
Labor Relations

MARKETING

Market Plan Formats
Merchandising
Product-line Development
Market Evaluation
Market Research
Sales Promotion

PERSONNEL/INDUSTRIAL RELATIONS

Industrial Relations
Recruitment/Employment
Labor Negotiations
Personnel Policies
Benefits Administration
Salary Administration
Employee Relations

PLANT MANAGEMENT

Production Methods
Union Negotiations
Production Control
Quality Control
Government Contracts
Industrial Engineering

PUBLIC RELATIONS

Educational Programs
Customer Relations
Public Relations
Liaison/Coordination
Meeting Arrangements
Press Releases

PURCHASING

Vendor Evaluation
Purchasing Management
Contracts
Problem Solving
Inventory Control

REAL ESTATE

Site Criteria
Market Analysis
Legal Documentation
Project Development
Leasing
Mortgage Financing
Sales/Brokerage

SALES/SALES MANAGEMENT

Sales Administration
Dealer Setup
Marketing
Brand Management
Sales Training
Sales Forecasting
National Account Contact
Personnel Selling Key Accounts

SOCIAL WORK

Vocational Counseling
Teaching
Staff Supervision
Program Development
Performance Evaluation
Office Administration

EDUCATION

First show the college or university granting your degree. Include your major and minor if they are a plus—that is, if they are related to your objective. If you received your degree after attending several colleges, list the degree-granting college first. Do not include colleges attended for only a short time. If you have no degree, begin your list of colleges attended with the school generally held in highest regard.

PROFESSIONAL MEMBERSHIPS AND CERTIFICATION

Include professional and trade association memberships pertinent to your work; extraneous listings just fill space. If you have a professional certification, such as CLU, CPA, or Registered Engineer, include this.

AVAILABILITY

If you are now employed, you must give notice. Thus, if thirty or sixty days' notice is required, say so. Avoid printing an exact date in your résumé. If unemployed, it is often best to omit this item.

PRESENT EMPLOYER CONTACT

This is a very important item. If you do not wish your present employer to be asked about you at this time, say so in your résumé. In circumstances in which your current boss knows that you are leaving, it can often be a big plus if he or she will give you a good send-off. In summary, it depends on whether your superior is aware that you are planning to change jobs and whether he or she will give you a good recommendation.

RELOCATION

If you are seeking a job in a field that might require you to relocate, then it is favorable to say so in your résumé. If you absolutely will not move for any reason, you might as well say that. (Say, "Prefer not to relocate" rather than "Will not relocate.") If the subject is an open one with you and your family, it is best to omit this item altogether.

PERSONAL DATA

As a rule of thumb, include what is beneficial to you or is generally looked upon as "normal." Remember, a potential employer will be impressed with what he or she thinks you can do for the organization. Factors such as youth, age, and sex are no longer given the importance they once had. If you think that your birthdate might be a negative, don't include it. (Exception: Executive search consultants really like to know your vital statistics.)

What do height and weight have to do with your anticipated contribution? Not much. Health problems can reasonably be a job factor. You should not lie about such a problem, but it may be best to omit it from your résumé. But if height, weight, age, and health are "normal" (whatever that is!), you won't go wrong by including them, probably as the last item in your résumé. If current trends continue into the future, the marital status of individuals may be changing with frequency, so include this or not, as you think best. The number and ages of your children are not vital to most jobs.

TRAVEL

If you know that extensive travel will be involved in your potential new job, you might as well express your willingness to travel as required. Otherwise, this is an item for your personal consideration, not for your résumé.

INTERESTS AND ACTIVITIES

If any of your hobbies or interests are truly relevant, this is a good résumé item, if space permits. Otherwise, remind yourself about them, but omit.

SERVICE TO YOUR COMMUNITY

Community service is generally not for the résumé, unless such service is a part of your job. Many executive positions require this kind of contribution, however, so if space permits and if the activities are relevant, include them in your résumé. At any rate, for your own knowledge, review what you've done in the way of community service in your present and past communities. This may be useful in interviews and as luncheon ice-breakers.

FOREIGN LANGUAGES

Do you speak, read, and/or write a foreign language? If you are not fluent, best to forget it. This is not for your résumé, unless pertinent to the sought-after job.

FOREIGN TRAVEL EXPERIENCE

Again, not for the résumé, unless past travel experience is a plus in the new position you are seeking.

MILITARY SERVICE

Exclude this from the résumé. If you've been in the Service and the subject comes up, use it in conversation.

BUSINESS REFERENCES

Do not use business references in the résumé. References change, as situations change. Personal references are almost never used, as they have little practical value. Business or professional references are essential, however. Arrange for these with individuals who know your contributions. Prepare a typed list of three or four, with names, titles, organizations, addresses, and phone numbers. You will probably only need half a dozen copies of this list (each individually typed), since references are generally only given at the request of the potential employer. There is no need to volunteer your list. If it appears that many copies will be needed, have them produced by a fast printer (see chapter 9 regarding copies, quality of printing, and paper). Never use carbon copies of your list. Carry your list with you at all times. Consider preparing separate lists with different individual references depending on your objective.

SALARY REQUIREMENTS

Never include salary requirements in your résumé, as it might cost you several thousand dollars. Decide in your own mind an acceptable range, subject to benefits and perks, and then negotiate after you have received a job offer. To repeat, *never* mention salary requirements in your résumé.

WORK EXPERIENCE/EMPLOYMENT HISTORY

Now that you have done the easy parts, what's next? The heart of your résumé, that's what. Start with plenty of blank paper for each job you have held. Begin in reverse chronological order, starting with your current or last position. Make a separate write-up for each position with each firm, agency, organization, or company.

Employer Name/Address/Description

Use the correct current name of the organization and a division or subsidiary if one is or was your employer. Show the approximate size in sales dollars or, depending on circumstances, the number of employees, units in a chain, members in an association, or the size of the annual budget in your governmental agency, institution, or not-for-profit foundation. Describe the activities very briefly, except for those employers whose names are either household words or self-explanatory.

Dates of Employment

Record these dates accurately, from and to, for your own information. For example: May 15, 1980–December 31, 1986. (On your actual résumé show years only, if at all feasible; e.g., 1980–1986 should suffice.) More precise dates can be given in an interview, should they be required.

Position Held

In most cases the position you held can best be described by using your personal title or the position title. Do not fabricate a fancy title if you didn't have one.

Earnings

Normally, earnings should not be listed in a résumé. Save this information for an interview, where it might be a factor in salary negotiations. Do, however, get your earnings down on paper to refresh your memory and in case you need the facts later.

In the upper brackets you might consider showing current or recent earnings to filter out any employers who might not realize where you stand in the salary hierarchy.

Responsibilities

Write out all of the responsibilities of each position, then put them in digest form. List the three, four, or five items of major importance. A brief sentence is all the space you can give to each one. Omit details. Refer to the sample résumés in chapter 6 to see how this is done.

Achievements

What did you do well in prior positions? Here again, as you look back over your career so far, ask yourself what counted most with regard to organizational goals reached, clients or customers satisfied, designs created, or sales or profits built. In other words, focus on those areas where you contributed, led the way, or carried out plans. What was your share of these achievements?

Again, see chapter 6 for examples to stimulate your thinking. Do not make big deals out of little deals. Don't exaggerate. Avoid "ego statements." In those positions in which there were no accomplishments, make no list. Concentrate on those positions, preferably more current ones, where you did produce. Always keep your job objective and/or career plan in mind as you search out your top contributions. Those achievements that relate to your objective will be most effective. All other materials are nice to read but may be extraneous. Do not pretend that apples are oranges. Employers have had a lot of experience, too.

How do you put such accomplishments in writing? First, get your material down on paper in draft form, as you review each prior work assignment. Then, write and rewrite until each of your achievements is concisely stated in one sentence, short but complete. Don't quit with that. See if you can restate each sentence so that if you were doing the hiring, you would be affected positively.

Are you finished now? Not quite. Review this section once more. Does each statement suggest a firm, confident individual, without excessive ego? More important, does it reflect you and what you are? Is the choice of words the best possible? You want to be careful here, for you are in the heart of your résumé. The employer is now thinking, "What did you do for others, that I hope you can do for me, to solve my problems, to fill my needs?"

As this handbook will remind you from time to time, a résumé has one principal, essential aim: to get you an interview. That's why what you write and how you write it are so important. They spell success or failure, whether you are directing your résumé to a potential employer, to an executive search recruiter, or to your contacts.

Reason for Change

It's best to omit any reference to why you left an employer or an assignment. There are some exceptions, but as a rule, it is almost impossible to state in a sentence or two why you left, whose decision it was, whose fault, or what the situation really was. No matter how you state a reason, you give an employer the opportunity to decide not to interview you based upon what he or she reads.

Never write in your résumé that you left by mutual agreement. Employers translate this into "fired." You will doubtless be asked for your reasons by every potential employer, but by omitting them from your résumé you will at least have the privilege of presenting each reason in favorable terms. Another benefit of giving no reasons for leaving in a résumé is that it keeps you honest. You can't be tempted to cover up, blame your ex-boss, or lie just a little.

Here are some reasons given (taken from actual résumés) that are presumably sincere and honest but are easily misinterpreted or viewed negatively by employers. The comment following each example suggests what a potential employer might think.

Resigned by mutual agreement, due to economic reversals requiring cutback.

He or she was fired or quit to avoid termination. The statement might or might not be true. Most "mutual agreements" are not instigated by the employee.

Resigned after completion of a leave of absence.

What's this all about? Why was a leave of absence taken?

No opportunity for further advancement under present management practices.

Could be true, probably is. But is this person simply dissatisfied? Why no advancement? Not promotable any more? Burnout?

Seek new opportunity to apply knowledge and experience.

This could mean almost anything. Of course, it could be a normal desire to climb higher. Was this turnover the fault of the employer or the employee?

If you strongly believe that the reason for changing your current or last job is logically justifiable and normally acceptable by employers, then you may safely use it for that position only. Examples of such situations would include a business or department being closed or relocated, a merger, resignation to have a family, or severe economic conditions causing a staff reduction. However, even under such circumstances, it may be best not to give a reason. If you include some reasons and not others, an employer is automatically interested in the reasons *not* given.

While there are pros and cons for including or excluding your reasons to change, experience strongly suggests that it is best to omit them and then discuss them openly and truthfully when asked in an interview.

At this stage you've done your homework on your work history. If you did it thoroughly you don't need to do it again. The data will enable you to write a sales-tool résumé and will better prepare you for any interview. Save your work papers and notes. You may need them again someday for a new résumé with a different objective.

5

Choosing Your Résumé Style

The Executive Résumé Handbook suggests four styles of résumés, each one subject to variations or combinations. Don't be too hasty to select the first one that appeals to you. Give the other styles some thought and look at the samples at the end of this chapter.

The basic résumé styles are: chronological, functional, achievement, and creative. (Your résumé could be in still another style should you run into one that pleases you more. Remember, though, that the key word is not "pleasing"; it is "effective.") Do not place undue importance on these four résumé styles. An employer doesn't care what category your executive résumé falls into. What matters is what you have to say and how well you say it.

The *chronological style* lists your work history in inverse order, with your current or last job shown first. Under each employer you normally show dates of employment, titles or positions, responsibilities, and accomplishments. This style may be more useful for a career continuation than for a career change. It might not be the best if you have been unemployed for a long time. Another reason for this format, which is used more than any other, is that it permits you to show growth in an organization, or in your career, or in both.

The *functional style* is useful if your career has been varied and leads toward your new objective. This format divides responsibilities or achievements by work functions or classifications. A favorite, and effective, way of presenting a successful work history is to use a page of achievements arranged by functions. Your accomplishments are organized under headings, with no mention made of employer names or employment dates.

The *achievement style* places all, or the major, highlights of your career at the top of page one of your résumé (right below your objective), showing what you did particularly well, in terms of goals reached or exceeded, in whatever your fields or positions. The listing is not necessarily by function, although it can be. No employer data is included on page one. A concise, usually abbreviated, history of employment follows. If you have been highly successful, the achievement style is often a good choice. This style is an effective interest-catching format, assuming that the reader picks up one or more items that are meaningful. Most readers never do get to page two if nothing on page one impresses them.

The *creative style* can take any form the writer can devise. One problem is that too much creativity may cover a lack of substance; employers know this and may be turned off. Once again, the purpose of a résumé is to gain an interview, not to demonstrate your writing talent.

A business or professional résumé *can* be creative, but such a style can be a questionable choice, as it probably is not what the reader is expecting. Exception: In artistic fields considerable license is acceptable, and in fact may be welcomed by an employer.

Which style should you use? The one that represents you best and that highlights your accomplishments for other employers. Remember, regardless of the style of your résumé, both style and format are secondary to content and good presentation of the salient facts. Let your chosen style be suitable to who you are and what you do.

ALTER D. DULLIMAN

20 Bumpstead Lane
urbank, CA 90671
hone: (213) 823-8812

ales and Management

-- Floor Covering or Related Home Furnishings Industry

SUMMARY A capable, productive Sales Executive with a vigorous, effective approach--thoroughly knowledgeable and experienced--combining high volume personal selling of major accounts with administrative ability and experience.

AREAS OF
KNOWLEDGE

Sales Administration	Product Line Development
Policy Determination	Pricing
Sales Forecasting	
	Sales Meetings
Personal Selling of Key Accounts	Trade Shows
Customer Relations	Sales Hiring, Training
	Sales Supervision, Motivation
Distribution	Territory Layout
Marketing	Compensation Plans
Merchandising	
Sales Promotion	Distributors, Wholesalers Manufacturers Representatives

EXPERIENCE
Feb., 1980
to Present

CARPET MASTER MILLS, Los Angeles, California

Position: Manager, Contract Division

Responsibilities:
-- To establish and implement a plan to increase the commercial carpet volume for the Company.
-- To personally build relationships with leading architects, leading to Company products being specified for large projects.
-- To direct the sales organization in contract activities.
-- To personally handle key contract accounts.

16

Achievements:
-- Sold 4 major school jobs within 60 days.
-- Initiated numerous potential sales to schools, hospitals, libraries, nursing homes and condominiums.
-- Have successfully motivated the sales staff to further productive effort in commercial work.

Oct., 1977
Sept., 1979

HOLLYWOOD CARPET MILLS, Los Angeles, California
Carpet manufacturers. Annual sales volume $32 million.

Position: Vice President Sales, Midwest Division, after promotion from Assistant to the President.

Responsibilities:
-- To prepare market plan formats and one year sales forecasts.
-- To have full sales responsibility for the Midwest Division.
-- To handle policy determination, organizational structure, market research and market potential evaluation.
-- To plan merchandising, sales promotion, pricing, and work on proprietary accounts.

Achievements:
-- Launched a marketing effort which increased sales 50%.
-- Led the sales force to acquire 150 new accounts in one year.
-- Increased market penetration by 20% through realignment of sales territories.
-- Directed 10 salesmen in 13 midwestern states plus an Operations Manager and a staff of 30 in a 50,000 sq. ft. warehouse.

Aug., 1973
Oct., 1977

CARPET-TEX OF CALIFORNIA, Los Angeles, California.
Carpet manufacturers. Annual sales volume $15 million.

Position: General Sales Manager, after promotion from Regional Manager and Contract Manager.

Responsibilities:
-- To increase sales, and number of distributors, through 2 Regional Managers and 18 salesmen in 11 Western States.
-- To enlarge contract business through direction of sales specialist.
-- To handle product research and development, and approve all new products.
-- To administer production of marketing data and sales reports.

Achievements:
-- Received three promotions within 3 years.
-- Led sales to 100% or more of all target figures.
-- Personally hired all but 2 of an effective 20-man staff.

1964
1973

BIGELOW RUGS AND CARPETS, New York, New York
Annual sales volume $100 million.

Positions: Sales Representative, in Los Angeles, Midwest and
            New York.

Responsibilities and Achievements:
-- To increase sales in assigned territories, through Depart-
   ment Stores, Specialty Stores, Contract business.
-- Continually met all assigned quotas.
-- Finished 1st in the U.S. one year, in % over quota.
-- Always finished among top 10 of 130 salesmen nationally.

1956
1964

PHILCO DISTRIBUTORS, INC., New York, New York

Position: Sales Representative

Responsibilities and Achievements:
-- To sell to Department and Appliance stores in New York
   City.
-- Produced sales increases in most assigned territories.

TRAVEL   Agreeable to amount required to handle the position success-
                fully.

LOCATE   Willing to consider relocating.

AVAILABILITY   Minimum of 2-3 weeks' notice required.

EMPLOYER   Present employer is not aware of decision to change and may
CONTACT   not be contacted at this time.

ERIC BENSINGER

7129 Horseshoe Lake Drive
Bassville, OH 44039
Phone: (216) 519-6518

OBJECTIVE | Plant Manager

AREAS OF
KNOWLEDGE
AND
EXPERIENCE

Production Methods	Mechanical Engineering
Testing and Evaluation	Machine Design
Production Control	
	Technical Management
Time and Motion Studies	Forecasts
Feasibility Studies	Specifications
Scheduling	Installation
Projections	Start-up
Cost Calculations	Maintenance
Inventory Control	Computer Usage
Loss and Scrap Control	Statistical Analysis

EDUCATION

Case Institute of Technology, Cleveland, Ohio
    B.S. Degree in Mechanical Engineering
        Major: Mechanical Design

Ohio University, Athens, Ohio
    MBS in Finance and Management

Special Training Courses: Motion Time Survey; Manufacturing
    Studies; Engineering Operations Course; Interpersonal
    Communications Workshop

PROFESSIONAL
MEMBERSHIPS

American Management Association
American Society of Mechanical Engineers

EXPERIENCE
Feb., 1978
to Present

GIANT U.S. MANUFACTURER

(March, 1983
to Present)

Position: Supervisor - Equipment Development
          Incandescent Lamp Department, Machine Design
          Cleveland, Ohio

Responsibilities:
-- Design and develop high-speed, proprietary lamp-making
   machinery; supervise a staff of 4 Engineers, 4 Design
   Specialists, 3 Designers and 2 Detailers.
-- Budget and forecast: design time, development expendi-
   ture, subsequent investment expenditures for machinery-
   related cost improvement and new product projects.
-- Control annual development expenditures of $400,000.
-- Serve as the Incandescent Lamp Department Representative
   to the Division; member of Technical Committee on Energy,
   Coiling Committee and Suggestion Board.

Achievements:
-- Maintained more than 5-year backlog of short-term payoff
   projects through imaginative approaches to automating
   manual operations and to improving productivity.
-- Increased technical depth of group by broadening individuals' areas of responsibility.
-- Recommended evaluation of high-temperature, non-corrosive,
   wear resistant and energy absorbing materials in numerous
   critical applications.
-- Reduced cost of material and fabrication by substituting
   plastics for metals in many areas.
-- Taught manufacturing studies courses in Manufacturing Engineering.

(Oct., 1979   Position: Manufacturing Project Engineer
Feb., 1983)   Lamp Plant - Circleville, Ohio

Responsibilities:
-- Complete responsibility for the transfer of all specialty
   fluorescent machinery and product lines from Cleveland
   Lamp Plant to Circleville Plant; total cost of transfer
   $250,000.
-- Handle plant layout, services, and the installation and
   debugging of $1.3 million in reprographic lamp making
   machinery.
-- Train hourly personnel in manual operations and maintenance.

Achievements:
-- Provided smooth start-up of specialty lamp manufacture in
   Circleville Plant.
-- Tuned reprographic equipment and trained operators to meet
   heretofore unknown quality standards.
-- Initiated productivity and scrap improvement projects
   totalling $100,000.

20

(Feb., 1978   Position: Manufacturing Project Engineer
Sept., 1979)   Lamp Plant - Cleveland, Ohio

Responsibilities:
-- Document methods and workplaces of manual operations with
   use of Motion Time Survey (predetermined time standards).

Achievements:
-- Contributed $120,000 in cost reduction through machine de-
   sign and methods improvements in a bench welding piecework
   area.
-- Designed, detailed, sub-contracted fabrication, and de-
   bugged fluorescent packaging station.

Feb., 1977   PARKER HANNIFIN, Engine Accessories Division, Cleveland, Ohio.
Jan., 1978

Positions: Buyer
           Production Planner

Responsibilities:
-- As Buyer: Purchase castings and stampings; handle MRO,
   sub-contracting, vendor audits.
-- As Production Planner: Schedule and expedite prototype
   fuel nozzles and valves through model shop fabrication
   and lab assembly.

Achievements:
-- Consistently met delivery and shipping schedules through
   persistent follow-up.
-- Contributed to cost improvement through EOQ investiga-
   tions.
-- Served as liaison with vendor in the purchase and quali-
   fication of Electron Beam Welder.

June, 1976   THE GOSS COMPANY, Chicago, Illinois
Jan., 1977

Position: Design Engineer

Responsibilities: Design and detail newspaper printing presses.

EMPLOYER   Present employer is not aware of decision to consider change
CONTACT   and may not be contacted at this time.

REFERENCES   Available upon request.

21

ERNEST P. MATTHEWS

3613 East Milford St.
Denver, CO 72588
Telephone: (303) 464-2035

OBJECTIVE   <u>Administrative Management</u>

                   -- Operations, Auditing, Financial

AREAS OF   <u>Accounting</u>
KNOWLEDGE   -- Experience as British Chartered Accountant includes:
AND   General, Public, Private, Finance, Liquidation and
EXPERIENCE   Foreign Exchange.

                   <u>Auditing</u>
                    -- Nine years Operations and Financial Auditing.
                    -- Assignments included multi-million dollar manufacturing
                       corporations.

                   <u>Operations Management</u>
                    -- Two years Management Claims Processing Operation.
                    -- Managing 150 personnel through 12 Supervisors.
                    -- Production, Inventory Control, Quality Control.
                    -- Interface with Zerodex System; involved in 2 conversions.
                    -- Handling $100 million in claims disbursement.
                    -- $1.5 million annual Operating Budget.
                    -- Conducted Management Development Program.

                   <u>Cost Settlement/Management Audits</u>
                    -- Three years third party reimbursement settlement audits.
                    -- Managing $1 million fee audit subcontracts.
                    -- Full-scope/limited-scope audits of hospitals in Colorado
                       and bordering states.
                    -- Complex reimbursement problems.
                    -- National Medicare appeal hearings.
                    -- Operations analysis work for hospitals on special assign-
                       ment.

                   <u>Insurance</u>
                    -- Third party reimbursement Federal programs.
                    -- Private sector administration of Federal contracts.

                   <u>Consumer Service</u>
                    -- Service Management
                    -- Expediting and Tracing
                    -- Complaints
                    -- Liaison with Marketing
                    -- Customer Correspondence

PERSONAL   Birthdate: 10-29-50   Married   5'11"   200 Lbs.

EDUCATION   City of London College, London, England
                     British Chartered Accountant Degree   Major: Accounting

22

PROFESSIONAL
CERTIFICATION
British Chartered Accountant (CPA Equivalent)

PROFESSIONAL
MEMBERSHIPS
Hospital Financial Management Association
Institute of Chartered Accountants in England and Wales.

EXPERIENCE
Nov., 1980
to Present

LEADING HEALTH INSURANCE COMPANY. Nation's largest private
carrier for health insurance. 3,000 employees

(Aug., 1984
to Present)

Position: Manager, Health Division Claims

Responsibilities:
-- Manage $100 million disbursement in claims payments per
   year.
-- Control a $1.5 million operating budget.
-- Manage 150 employees through 12 Supervisors.
-- Maintain work inventories at target levels for volume, age
   and cycle time; maintain quality standards.

Achievements:
-- Reduced cost per claim processing from $4.10 to $2.85 in
   12 months.
-- Eliminated all national claims and inquiry backlogs between
   August, 1984 and March, 1985.
-- Attained National performance standards and goals as re-
   gards inventory, size, age and production cycle times.
-- Participated in 2 successful computer conversions.
-- Reorganized and reduced personnel, saving approximately
   $150,000 per year.
-- Improved productivity by introduction of work measurement
   as a management tool.
-- Developed subordinate management personnel.
-- Incorporated 3 additional claims processing functions in
   1985 while remaining within original dollar budget.

(Nov., 1980
Aug., 1984)

Position: Manager of Auditing, Health Division, after promo-
          tions from Auditor positions.

Responsibilities:
-- Responsible for out-of-state subcontracts, specifically up
   to $1 million contracts for Nebraska, Kansas, and other
   regional health plans.
-- Managed 25 professional personnel through 3 Supervisors.
-- Responsible for negotiating cost settlements with contracting Hospital providers (hospitals, skilled nursing facilities and home health agencies).

Sept., 1974   TOWNSEND & COMPANY (INTERNATIONAL), London, England
July, 1980   Chartered accountants; 250 employees.

                 <u>Position</u>: Senior Auditor, after promotions from Junior
                          Auditor and Trainee

                 <u>Responsibilities and Achievements</u>:
                 -- Audits of private and public corporations; management
                    consulting.
                 -- Handle taxation, liquidations, investigations, stock
                    valuations.
                 -- Progressed to responsibility for concurrent multi-audits,
                    including a number of the firm's largest clients.
                 -- Discovered cases of fraud in client companies.

                 <u>Reason for Change</u>: Moved to the U.S. for permanent residence.

TRAVEL   Agreeable to moderate travel including overseas.

LOCATION   Willing to relocate.

AVAILABILITY   3-4 weeks' notice required.

EMPLOYER   Present employer is not aware of decision to consider change
CONTACT   and may <u>not</u> be contacted at this time.

FOREIGN
LANGUAGE   French: read and write; speak moderately well.

FOREIGN   Extensive travel in Western and Eastern Europe, Russia, and
TRAVEL   Canada

GORDON N. BAKER

17 Rhododendron Drive
Raleigh, NC 35129
Telephone: (919) 549-5206

OBJECTIVE   Sales Management or Sales

HIGHLIGHTS   As National Sales Director
OF
CAREER   .. Developed innovative approaches to selling department
                stores.
             .. Initiated a Company weekly Idea Clearing House bulletin
                which has achieved recognition as most stimulating in-house
                merchandising tool.
             .. High level presentations created major accounts: Wickes
                Furniture; Gimbels, Pittsburgh; Jones Store, Kansas City;
                Kaufman's, Pittsburgh.

             As National Accounts Manager

             .. Increased annual sales to one account from $600,000 (1984)
                to $2.5 million (Year 1985).
             .. Developed unique marketing approach for Goodman which made
                use of both manufacturer and distributor names on merchan-
                dise for the first time.
             .. Built total national account program by 30% in 1984 through
                new merchandising and advertising.

             As District Marketing Manager

             .. Expanded sales from $2.3 million (Jan., 1982) to $3.1 mil-
                lion (December, 1983).
             .. Company's advertising exposure increased 50% in Chicago
                market; became dominant supplier for two major accounts.
             .. Successfully handled key major accounts: Dayton's, Gimbels,
                Carson Pirie Scott, Milwaukee Boston, Prange.

             As Territory Sales Representative
             .. Built New England sales from $769,000 (1977) to $2 million
                (1981).
             .. Added key major accounts in Hartford, Rochester, Long Is-
                land.
             .. Increased number of newspaper ads in New England over 25%.
             .. Successfully handled key major accounts: Forbes & Wallace,
                G. Fox, The Outlet Company, Sibley's, Fortunoff.

             As Salesman:
             .. Consistent sales leader in the District.
             .. Increased sales 20% per year for 2 years; exceeded all
                quotas.
             .. Rated No. 1 in District in building mail order sales.

```
EXPERIENCE
SUMMARY
Jan., 1984          GOODMAN FURNITURE COMPANY, Raleigh, NC
to Present          Furniture manufacturer. Sales volume $200 million.

(Sept., 1984        Position: National Sales Director
to Present)
                    Responsibilities:
                    .. Help develop and administer Goodman merchandising market-
                       ing programs nationally.
                    .. Chairman, Sales Manager's Committee and Member, Marketing
                       Committee which determine national marketing policies.
                    .. With Advertising Department, develop sales promotion and
                       advertising plans, including sales training films and aids.
                    .. Make presentations to major accounts at highest corporate
                       levels.
                    .. Publish merchandising ideas bulletins.

(Jan., 1984         Position: National Accounts Manager
Sept., 1984)
                    Responsibilities:
                    .. Represent 35 licensed factories to major national accounts;
                       develop merchandising and marketing policies.
                    .. Administer retail and wholesale pricing.
                    .. Develop sales promotional ideas for major accounts; make
                       top-level presentations.

Oct., 1977          WILKINS & LESTER, Cincinnati, Ohio. Manufacturers of mat-
Dec., 1983          tresses and diversified products. Sales volume $75 million.

(Jan., 1982         Position: District Marketing Manager
Dec., 1983)
                    Responsibilities:
                    .. Create and implement marketing policies for Midwest Dis-
                       trict; administer pricing, retail and wholesale.
                    .. Sell major department stores and furniture stores in a
                       4-state Midwest area.
                    .. Develop advertising/promotional ideas for major department
                       stores.
                    .. Improve merchandise displays; conduct floor salesmen educa-
                       tion programs; maintain store stock control programs.
                    .. Coordinate major account newspaper advertising.
                    .. Counsel department store Advertising Departments on tech-
                       niques of mattress advertising.

(Oct., 1977         Position: Territory Sales Representative
Jan., 1982)

March, 1975         BRYMAN & KESNER, Columbus, Ohio. Manufacturers of mattresses
Oct., 1977          and diversified products. Sales volume $170 million.

                    Position: Salesman

PERSONAL            Birthdate: 3-10-51     Married, Two children
```

ALLEN L. McARTHUR

1120 Valley Road
Bayview, MO 64162
Phone: (314) 286-5232

OBJECTIVE   <u>Senior Financial Management: Vice President, Treasurer</u>

HIGHLIGHTS   <u>For a Manufacturer: Sales in Excess of $100 Million</u>
OF
FINANCIAL   .. Established a short-term investing program; reduced cash
MANAGEMENT   balances by $500,000.
CAREER   .. Instituted a service charge program for receivables; re-
                duced days outstanding from 59 to 48 in first year (value -
                $2 million); produced revenues of $71,000 per year.
             .. Assisted in the listing of stock on the New York and Mid-
                west Stock Exchanges; worked with the specialist firms of
                the two Exchanges.
             .. Placed $8 million loan direct with an insurance company;
                saved placement fee.
             .. Changed carriers for workmen's compensation and liability
                insurance coverage; prevented deductible from being
                quadrupled.
             .. Arranged financing of a foreign subsidiary through a U.S.
                bank.
             .. Set up an employee investment plan in Company stock.
             .. Contributed to improved sales and collections by arranging
                a leasing company floor plan for financing equipment.
             .. Developed financing with Industrial Revenue Bonds in 2
                states.

AREAS OF   Financial Management   Long Range Planning
KNOWLEDGE   Short Term Financing   Profit Planning
AND   Long Term Financing
EXPERIENCE   Acquisition Analysis
             Financial Projections   Appraisals
             Cash Management
             Investments   Insurance
             Financial Analysis   Credit and Collection
                                           Records Retention
             Bank Relations   Profit Sharing Plans
             Stockholder Relations   Leasing
             Financial Institution Contact

EDUCATION   University of Missouri, Columbia, Missouri - 4 years
                B.S. Degree in Business Administration

             Special Training: American Management Association Seminars
                International Trade and Finance; Financial Management;
                Corporate Insurance Management; Credit and Collection;
                Cash Forecasting; Operations Research; Sales Forecasting

27

EXPERIENCE
SUMMARY
1965 to
Present

TEMPLE ELECTRIC CO., Triston, Missouri. Subsidiary of Emerson Electric Co., St. Louis. Manufacturer; sales volume $175 million.

Financial/Planning Positions:
    Vice President, Planning (Oct., 1985 to Present)
    Treasurer (1981-1985)
    Assistant Treasurer (1977-1981)

Responsibilities:
-- As Chief Financial Officer, full responsibility for cash management, forecasts and projections.
-- Plan and handle short-term financing; arrange long-term financing through insurance company, industrial revenue bonds and banks.
-- Maintain good personal relations with all financial institutions.
-- Work with Company's financial relations firm.
-- Manage credit and collection; control accounts receivable; place Company insurance; handle leasing.
-- Locate and review companies for possible acquisition; arrange appraisals.
-- As Vice President, Planning, work on long-range plans with 2 subsidiaries and 4 Divisions; follow through on implementation and monitor the results.

Prior Positions with the Company:
    Manager, Market Services (1977)
    Manager, Market Research (1975-1977)
    Supervisor, Market Research (1970-1974)
    Market Analyst (1966-1970)
    Sales Statistician (1965-1966)

Reason to Change: Desire to return to the finance area of business; Company merged in May, 1986, and principal Treasury functions transferred to parent corporate headquarters.

PERSONAL

Birthdate: 12-3-38   Married, Two children
5'8"   160 Lbs.   Excellent health

TRAVEL

Agreeable to travel required; home on weekends.

LOCATION

Willing to relocate.

AVAILABILITY

30 days' notice required.

EMPLOYER
CONTACT

Present employer is not aware of decision to consider change and may not be contacted at this time.

REFERENCES

Available upon request.

ALBERT W. NEUBERGER

3617 College Avenue
Paterson, NJ 10768
Telephone: (201) 719-7617

OBJECTIVE

Production Management/Plant Management

HIGHLIGHTS
OF
PRODUCTION
CAREER

As Production Manager: Nine-Year Period

.. Expanded manufacturing operation from 50,000 units per year to 880,000 units in 9 years.
.. Increased production by 35% over previous standard.
.. Achieved 25% increase in plant efficiency based on production man hours.
.. Established time and price rates which resulted in higher net profit for Company.
.. Saved $130,000 a year by increasing inventory turnover; 1977-1986.
.. Reduced production backlog by 40,000 units in 1-1/2 years; 4-month lag to zero.
.. Saved $25,000 per year by developing internal controls for last-in-shop materials.
.. Reduced machine down time from 12% to .05%.
.. Reduced reject-reworking time by 40% by upgrading the caliber of employees through an effective efficiency rating system.
.. Reduced returns from 5% to 1-1/2%.
.. Established formal training procedures for all new machine operations.

As Production Supervisor: Ten-Year Period

.. Improved productivity by engineering and procedures changes; increased production total from 3 units per man/day to 8.
.. Contributed substantially to engineering development on both product design and fixture design.
.. Progressed from Stockman to Supervisor in 5 years; one of the youngest Supervisors in the plant; consistently earned 100% of maximum bonus.

AREAS OF
KNOWLEDGE
AND
EXPERIENCE

Production Management
Production Planning
Production Scheduling
Staff Supervision
Quality Control
Inventory Control
Purchasing
Cost Control
Engineering
Factory Layout

Product Development
Traffic
Warehousing
Shipping, Receiving
Personnel Hiring
Supervisory Training
Personnel Records
Customer Consulting
Customer Complaints

PROFESSIONAL
MEMBERSHIP

National Association of Purchasing Agents

29

EDUCATION	Triton Junior College, Paterson, New Jersey Major: Business Administration
EXPERIENCE Feb., 1977 to Present	ELECTROWARE, INC., Beloit, NJ. Manufacturers of electrical hardware. Sales volume $15 million; 135 employees.

Position: Production Manager

Responsibilities:
  -- Manage all plant operations; production and warehousing.
  -- Direct production planning and scheduling.
  -- Hire and train supervisory and factory personnel.
  -- Maintain inventory control and cost control.
  -- Manage quality control from production to finished
     products.

1967 1977	NEW ENGLAND ELECTRIC COMPANY, Newark, NJ Manufacturers of communications equipment.

Position: Production Supervisor

Responsibilities:
  -- Manage production assembly, including production schedul-
     ing.
  -- Supervise up to 40 line employees.
  -- Assign work; handle instruction and training.
  -- Recommend and implement engineering changes.
  -- Make time studies.
  -- Maintain inventory control.
  -- Work on product design and prototype development.
  -- Handle repairs and returns.

Feb., 1964 Sept., 1966	UNITED STATES NAVY

Position: Damage Control Engineer 3rd Class

SALARY	Open to discussion.
TRAVEL	Agreeable to any travel required by the position.
LOCATION	Prefer Eastern area for the present; willing to consider re-locating in the future.
AVAILABILITY	30-60 days' notice required.
EMPLOYER CONTACT	Present employer is not aware of decision to consider change and may not be contacted at this time.

GEORGE T. COLLINS, Ph.D.

9427 So. Evergreen
Chicago, IL 60645
Phone: (312) 527-6219

POSITION SOUGHT	<u>Research Scientist</u>
OBJECTIVE	To conduct and direct independent, long range research in information retrieval and related areas.
SUMMARY	An established information scientist with a record of successful research experience and publications in the fields of information retrieval, mechanical translation, logic and linguistics, and related programming techniques.

AREAS OF RESEARCH EXPERIENCE

Information Retrieval:
   Retrieval System Design
   Retrieval System Evalua-
      tion
   Indexing Theory
   Question-answering Systems
   Computer Storage Techniques

Mathematical Linguistics
   Theory of Syntax
   Theory of Semantics

Mathematical Logic

Mechanical Translation

PERSONAL

Birthdate: 4-10-50   Married, Family
6'   165 Lbs.   Excellent Health

CITIZENSHIP

Canadian with permanent U.S. visa. Expect to become United States citizen

EDUCATION

The Principia College, Elsah, Illinois; B.A. Degree
M.I.T., Cambridge, Massachusetts; M.Sc. Degree in Mathematics
University of California, Berkeley, California; Ph.D. Degree
    in Logic and Methodology of Science

PROFESSIONAL ASSOCIATIONS

American Association for Advancement of Science
American Society for Information Science
Association for Machine Translation and Computational Lin-
    guistics
Association for Symbolic Logic
Linguistic Society of America

CITATION LISTINGS

"American Men of Science"
"Who's Who in the Computer Field"

EXPERIENCE	
1981 to Present	**LEADING MIDWEST PRIVATE UNIVERSITY**

<u>Title</u>: Assistant Professor of Information Science

<u>Responsibilities and Achievements</u>:
-- Co-principal investigator for each of two separate con-currently conducted long-term research projects under National Science Foundation Grants. (Project titles: "A Requirements Study for Future Library Catalogs" and "Studies in Indexing Depth and Retrieval Effectiveness.")
-- Member of two editorial boards (Journal Titles: <u>Mechanical Translation and Computational Linguistics</u> and <u>The Library Quarterly</u>).
-- Regular contributing reviewer for <u>Zentralblatt der Mathematik</u>.
-- Originated and developed new graduate courses in information science.
-- Directed graduate research in several areas of information science.
-- Originated a number of new techniques in retrieval system design and evaluation.

1984
(short term leave of absence)

UNIVERSITY OF CALIFORNIA, Berkeley, California

<u>Title</u>: Visiting Assistant Professor of Information Science

<u>Responsibilities</u>:
-- Conducted research and taught seminar on methods of retrieval system evaluation.

1976-1983
(intermittent)

IBM RESEARCH LABORATORY, San Jose, California

<u>Position</u>: Research Scientist and Consultant
(Part-time research position during 1976-79 while earning Ph.D. Degree.)

1979-1980

UNIVERSITY OF ERLANGEN, West Germany

<u>Title</u>: Alexander von Humboldt Research Fellow

<u>Nature of Position</u>: Post-doctoral fellowship awarded to out-standing foreign scholars by a government-supported German research foundation.

<u>Achievements</u>: Independent research in the foundations of lan-guage and logic, leading to technical and popular publications.

| 1974-1976 | MECHANOLINGUISTICS PROJECT, University of California, Berkeley, California. |

Title: Research Assistant

Nature of Work: Part-time research position while taking courses leading to Ph.D.

| 1973-1974 | MECHANICAL TRANSLATION GROUP, M.I.T., Cambridge, Mass. |

Title: Research Assistant

Nature of Work: Part-time independent research while working toward Master's degree.

PUBLICATIONS	Please see attached bibliography.
LOCATION	Readily willing to relocate anywhere.
REFERENCES	Excellent references available immediately upon request.

GARY BARTHOLEMEW

1609 North Bridewell, St. Paul, MN 55429
(612) 352-1158   Age 45   Married

CAREER OBJECTIVE

Financial Executive

EDUCATION

Certified Public Accountant
MBA, BBA University of Michigan

BUSINESS EXPERIENCE

Sept., 1982
to Present

Nationwide Special Risk Insurance Organization, Minneapolis

Vice President and Treasurer (formerly Controller)

Parent company operates four insurance companies, two agency-
   brokerage companies and a small leasing company. Fifteen
   nationwide offices.

Responsibilities:

Accounting and EDP departments (70 employees)
Management and investment of working funds
Member of management committee
Secretary of investment committee

Accomplishments:

Developed financial reports to meet the needs of management
Increased profit awareness throughout the company
Trained assistants to be innovative, flexible leaders with
   emphasis on getting the job done -- correctly and on time
Set up money-saving accounting procedures and established
   vital new and timely computer end results

Jan., 1980
to
Sept., 1982

BASTION AND COMPANY, St. Paul, MN Chemicals

Internal Auditor

Conducted and assisted in operational audits of various divisions which resulted in savings of distribution and other
   costs

Phosphochem Division, Inc., Bartow, Florida.
  Division of Bastion and Company sold to
  Merichem Corporation in 1983.

Controller, Florida operations (phosphate mines and chemical
  plants)

Increased participation of financial group in management and
  decision making (controllership new position)

Improved cost analysis, budgeting and control of purchasing,
  capital and maintenance expenditures.

Nov., 1973   Coopers & Lybrand, 222 South Riverside Plaza, Chicago
to
Jan., 1980   Senior Auditor

Directed financial audits with emphasis on evaluation of pro-
  cedures and controls
Audited companies in variety of industries
Prepared tax returns, financial statements, SEC reports.

Mar., 1970   Somnor Petroleum Corporation, 380 Madison Avenue, New York
to   American Overseas Petroleum, Ltd. Somnor subsidiary.
Sept., 1973

Analyzed financial reports and budgets of foreign operating
  companies
Initial training included 18 months at Middle East and Far
  East oil installations.

PROFESSIONAL AFFILIATIONS
American Institute of Certified Public Accountants
Minnesota Society of Certified Public Accountants

REFERENCES
Professional and personal references furnished upon request.

EDWIN C. BRUMAY

4322 Linden Drive
Odessa, OH 42307
Telephone: (821) 922-1814 (Home)
          (821) 248-8479 (Office)

OBJECTIVE   President, Vice President, General Manager

GENERAL   Very broad, including responsible positions in General Manage-
EXPERIENCE   ment at both the Corporate and Division Levels. Profit re-
                   sponsibility for both a group of diversified manufacturing
                   companies and a single Division. Have managed all phases of
                   business activity: marketing, production and engineering,
                   accounting, and industrial relations.

                   Although primary business function has been operations during
                   the last six years, have also been involved in an aggressive
                   acquisition program, directed liquidations, negotiated the
                   sale of a company, and have been on both sides of mergers.

                   Profit minded, cost conscious, and people oriented, and have
                   been successful in providing motivation and leadership. A
                   self-starter, enjoy problem solving, and communicate well. A
                   generalist, with a good record of achievement due to involve-
                   ment in the daily operating details of each Division.

BUSINESS   ALSTEEL CORPORATION, Detroit (1975 to present)
EXPERIENCE
                   Position: Vice President   Compensation: $92,500 plus

                   Responsibilities: Total profit and operations responsibility for
                   a group of three diverse companies with a total annual sales of
                   almost $55 million. This group is quite profitable and engaged
                   in manufacturing: two Divisions in steel and aluminum metal
                   working industries and one Division involved in the paper
                   industry.

                   In addition to Group supervision duties, have successfully
                   served as the General Manager of all of the Divisions at various
                   times during the last six years.

                   Achievements: Have been with Alsteel Corporation, and an ac-
                   quired company, since 1975. Advancements within the Corpora-
                   tion have been earned through performance: from Controller of
                   two Divisions, to Vice President of a Subsidiary to Assistant
                   Group Manager, to Group Manager, to Corporate Vice President in
                   January, 1981.

Sales and earnings of the group have risen substantially during the past five years. Sales have increased over 50% during this period and earnings for 1983 and 1984 were at all-time highs due mainly to good market penetration, upgrading of some key personnel, and development of a team spirit. Morale and enthusiasm are high and the lines of communication are open. Attainable goals and budgets have been established and the majority of them have been met or exceeded.

Involved with the daily problems and projects at all three Divisions and have a close working relationship with the General Managers. This involvement and exposure has been excellent experience in preparation for a Chief Executive Officer position.

PRIOR BUSINESS EXPERIENCE	President: CENTER DEVELOPMENT CORPORATION and EDWIN BROS. & COMPANY, Indianapolis, Indiana (1972-1975) Co-founder of both firms engaged in residential and light commercial construction.
	Vice President: BOSTER DEVELOPMENT CORP., and affiliated companies, Indianapolis, Indiana (1969-1972) Vice President of Operations
	Controller: GART AND BLANK, INC., Michigan City, Indiana (1965-1969)
	Accountant: PRICE WATERHOUSE & CO., Chicago, Illinois (1963-1965)
PERSONAL	Birthdate: July 24, 1939 Married Excellent Health Three children
EDUCATION	Indiana University BS Degree in Business Administration - 1963
REFERENCES	References available upon request.
EMPLOYER CONTACT	Present employer is not aware of decision to consider a change and may not be contacted at this time.

6

Executive/Professional Résumé Samples

ALVIN J. WARNER

500 North Wexell Avenue
Elk Grove Village, IL 60007
Telephone: Home   (312) 498-6642
            Office (312) 658-0679

OBJECTIVE   <u>Patent Attorney with Law Firm</u>

                 Leading to Partnership

HIGHLIGHTS   * Filed over 30 patent applications per year covering: cata-
OF   lyst and processes for refining petroleum, oil and fuel addi-
BACKGROUND   tives, fertilizers, catalyst and equipment for reducing auto
                   emissions, instruments, textile equipment, oil burners, waste
                   water treating processes and equipment.

                 * Established competence in appellate practice before Board of
                   Appeals in U.S. Patent Office; filed 10 appeal briefs in 1982
                   and presented a number of oral arguments.

                 * Established competence in license negotiations and drafting;
                   from 1/3 to 1/2 time devoted to licensing activities, with
                   licenses involving multi-million dollar projects; negotiated and
                   drafted instrument and special device licenses.

                 * Established in cooperation with top management of subsidiary
                   company an international franchise/license program involving
                   agricultural technique to increase productivity of sandy soils.
                   Traveled to Egypt with company vice president to negotiate with
                   government.

                 * Participated in settlement of litigation where substantial lump
                   sum royalty was paid; have current litigation responsibility
                   where potential liability exceeds $10 million; consulted with
                   trial counsel in preparing interrogatories, answers to interro-
                   gatories, briefs and participated in depositions.

AREAS OF   Patent Law
KNOWLEDGE   Draft and prosecute U.S. and foreign patent applications
                      (chemical, mechanical, electrical).
                   Negotiate and draft license agreements.
                   Patent Litigation
                   Interference Practice
                 Trademark Law
                   Prepare and prosecute U.S. and foreign trademark applications.
                   Negotiate and draft franchise agreements.
                 Trade Secret Law
                   Negotiate and draft secrecy agreements.
                 Anti-trust and Unfair Competition Law

EDUCATION	John Marshall Law School, Chicago
	  J.D. Degree - 1975 (6th in class)
	Lawyer's Institute, John Marshall Law School
	  Substantive patent law, patent office practice, licenses and contracts, foreign patent law, anti-trust law, unfair competition-FTC practice, interference practice.
	Continuing Legal Education Seminars at John Marshall Law School,
	Practicing Law Institute, Patent Resources Group:
	  drafting patent applications, drafting licenses, patent anti-trust conflicts.
	St. Thomas College, St. Paul, Minnesota
	  B.S. Degree - 1972 Major: Chemistry

PROFESSIONAL
CERTIFICATION
MEMBERSHIPS
	Illinois Supreme Court, Court of Customs and Patent Appeals,
	  U.S. Patent Office
	American Bar Association, American Patent Law Association,
	  Patent Law Association of Chicago.

EXPERIENCE 1978 to Present	LEADING U.S. OIL COMPANY Position: Patent Attorney Responsibilities: -- Counsel management in industrial property matters such as acquisition and sale of technology. -- Prepare license agreements, trade secret agreements, patent applications. -- Prepare validity and infringement opinions. -- Recommend outside counsel for certain application work; review and critique such work. Reason to Change: To enter private practice of patent law.
1975 1978	ADDRESSOGRAPH-MULTIGRAPH CORPORATION, BRUNING DIVISION, Mt. Prospect, Illinois Position: Patent Attorney Responsibilities: -- Prepare and prosecute U.S. and foreign patent applications covering: photoelectrostatic and diazo copying arts, including machines, optical devices, electro-mechanical devices, electronic circuits, compositions of matter, coated copy papers. -- Prepare and prosecute U.S. and foreign trademark applications. -- Prepare validity and infringement opinions.
EMPLOYER CONTACT	Present employer is not aware of decision to consider change and may not be contacted at this time.

BARRY A. PUTNAM

39 Wynn Drive
Wood Lakes, CN 01172
Phone: (201) 445-4677

OBJECTIVE   Internal Audit Director: Major Corporation

             -- Management, Operations, Financial

HIGHLIGHTS   * Broad operational and financial auditing background with major
OF   corporations: Tobacco, Food Processing, Chemicals and Metals,
BACKGROUND   Truck Manufacturing, Public Utility, Office Machines and Equip-
               ment, Business Service, Conglomerates.

             * Successfully organized internal audit functions to handle co-
               ordinated financial and operational audits in diversified cor-
               porate activities in the U.S. and abroad.

             * Reduced public accounting fees for 6 large corporations; saved
               between $50,000 and $125,000 annually in each case.

             * Developed data which saved $1 million in a newly acquired
               Columbian subsidiary.

             * Revised logic of inventory control system which saved $200,000
               in system design costs.

             * Improved overall financial controls through financial and ope-
               rational audit for a Fortune 500 company, covering offices/
               plants in Europe, South America and the Far East.

             * Supplied data which saved $200,000 in sales proceeds of a
               foundry.

             * Standardized the public accounting scope and performance of
               worldwide audits.

AREAS OF   Internal Operational Auditing   General Accounting
KNOWLEDGE   Internal Financial Auditing   Responsibility Accounting
             Management Reporting   Cost Accounting
                                              Foreign Accounting
             Corporate Organization   Public Accounting
             Financial Management
             Budgets, Forecasts   Inventory Control
             Systems and Procedures   Production Control

             Office Operations   Staff Supervision
             Data Processing   Hiring
             Credit and Collection   Training

41

PERSONAL	Birthdate: 8-10-36 Married, Family 6' 200 Lbs. Excellent Health

EDUCATION	St. John's University, New York, NY - Evening Division - 8 yrs.
	  B.B.A. Degree - 1964
	  Major: Accounting Minor: Economics

COMPANY
AFFILIATIONS

<u>Senior Audit Management</u>

LARGE DIVERSIFIED FOOD PROCESSOR & DISTRIBUTOR, New York, NY

<u>Position</u>: Internal Control Consultant   Current Employer

CONSOLIDATED EDISON, New York, New York. Public Utility.
Annual volume $2.3 billion.

<u>Position</u>: Audit Director

KMS INDUSTRIES, INC., Ann Arbor, Michigan. 25-company conglomerate. Annual volume $250 million.

<u>Position</u>: Director of Audits and
          Management Services

SPERRY RAND-REMINGTON RAND DIVISION, New York, New York.
Office machines and equipment. Annual volume $600 million.

<u>Position</u>: Director of Internal Audits

DUN & BRADSTREET, INC., New York, New York. Business information and credit services. Annual volume $300 million.

<u>Position</u>: Group Auditing Manager

MACK TRUCKS, INC., Allentown, Pennsylvania. Truck manufacturer,
sales and service. Annual volume $300 million.

<u>Position</u>: Manager of Corporate Audits.

FOREIGN
TRAVEL

Extensive travel in Central America, South America, North
America, Australia, Europe.

CAROL FERRIS

5610 South Blanchard
Chicago, IL 60621
Telephone: (312) 856-1966

| OBJECTIVE | **Management Position** |
| | -- Product Line or Service Development |

AREAS OF
KNOWLEDGE
AND
EXPERIENCE

Finance
Profit and Strategic
  Planning
Statement Analysis
Cash Flow Projections
Cost Analysis
Management Reporting

Sales
Product Management
Product Pricing
Promotion
Account Representative
Sales Training
Sales Seminars Design

Data Processing/Time Sharing

Financial System Design
Operations Research
User Training
Vendor Bid Analysis

Languages: Fortran, Basic,
  GPSS, IAL
Software Evaluation
Systems and Procedures Manuals

EDUCATION

University of Illinois, Urbana, Illinois
  MBA Degree - 1978
Chicago Teachers College, Chicago
  Bachelor of Education Degree - 1974
Special Training
  AMA: Planning Cash Flows, Public Fund Accounting
  D & B: Credit Analysis

EXPERIENCE
1978 to
Present

(1984 to
Present)

MAJOR CHICAGO LOOP BANK

Position: Product Manager

Responsibilities:
-- Develop, market and implement new banking services for the
   senior management of $25-$150 million banks.
-- Assist in maintaining the current level of operations for
   existing customers of the Division; provide personal liaison
   on an independent basis, as needed.
-- Maintain appropriate reports to management on the status of
   current customers, financial services and products, and the
   need for development/refinement of current services or new
   market areas.

Achievements:
-- Developed a successful semi-annual Profit Planning Work-
   shop for executive officers of customer banks; designed
   appropriate sales and marketing material for the workshop
   "image."
-- Initiated the development of three additional workshops:
   Personnel Planning, Marketing, Pricing.
-- Sold existing services and workshops to the highest level
   of management in customer's organization: Senior Vice
   Presidents, Presidents, Chairmen.
-- Designed and implemented a statistical analysis program on
   salary expectations.
-- As Account Representative, supervised the transfer of cur-
   rent customers through 4 computer conversions.
-- Worked with the financial officers of customers in the de-
   velopment of cash flow analysis using time-sharing programs.

(1982-1984)   Position: Financial Engineer

Responsibilities:
-- Handle program testing, documentation, enhancements and
   pricing of services.
-- Create and develop new program ideas in the time-sharing
   computer environment.
-- Provide service, education and training to customers in
   using programs and physical hardware.
-- Increase sales to existing customers; develop new markets.

Achievements:
-- Designed and implemented a seminar on financial forecasting
   for partners and senior management of "Big Eight" Account-
   ing firms and representative smaller firms.
-- Assisted in the system design of the following: Accounts
   Payable, Budget Reporting, Inventory Control, Insurance
   Premium Accounting.
-- Implemented sales and servicing of the systems; set up of
   cost analysis, pricing, contract design, customer training
   manuals, and management reports on current operations.
-- Developed new market areas, i.e., park districts and muni-
   cipalities, through extensions of the capabilities of the
   Accounts Payable and Budget Reporting systems.

(1978-1982)   Position; Financial Analyst

Responsibilities:
-- Work independently to design research procedures, write
   computer programs, validate results and prepare reports on
   projects for top managements of various departments.
-- Assist in the presentation of the time-sharing concept to
   top bank management; train line management.

44

Achievements:
-- Completed independent Operations Research Projects in financial areas.
-- Conducted meetings and training programs for all levels of management on the use and sale of time-sharing bank software.
-- Assumed full responsibility for customer servicing and training in the use of the time-sharing programs: Bond Portfolio Accounting and Pricing, Capital Evaluation, Statistical Analysis, Trust Accounting.
-- Set up procedures for supervising and training new Division personnel in the programs offered to customers.

1978   UNIVERSITY OF ILLINOIS, Urbana, Illinois. Research Assistant.

1974   CHICAGO BOARD OF EDUCATION. Certified Teacher - 6th Grade.

TRAVEL   Agreeable to any normal travel required in the Chicago Metropolitan area.

EMPLOYER   Present employer is not aware of decision to consider change and
CONTACT   may not be contacted at this time.

PROFESSIONAL   National Association of Bank Women
MEMBERSHIPS   National Association of Black Professional Women

PERSONAL   Birthdate: 9-14-51   Married: Two children
                5'6"   130 Lbs.   Excellent Health

COMMUNITY   Illinois Children's Home and Aid Society
SERVICE   Professional Women's Auxiliary of Provident Hospital

REFERENCES   Available upon request.

CATHERINE L. GARDNER

2411 18th Street
Minneapolis, MN 55439
Telephone: (448) 793-8544

OBJECTIVE   Collection Management

AREAS OF   Collection Management   Interviewing
KNOWLEDGE   Credit Management   Hiring
AND   Establishing Objectives   Training
EXPERIENCE   Credit Investigation   Wage Reviews
                   Financial Analysis   Performance Reviews
                   Accounts Receivable
                   Data Processing Usage   Retail, Consumer

EXPERIENCE
1966 to   LEADING MIDWEST MAIL ORDER HOUSE
Present   Major mail order and mass merchandiser. Annual sales volume
                   $400 million; 12,000 employees.

(1983 to   Position: District Collection Manager
Present
  and   Responsibilities:
1970-1980)   -- Supervise 8 to 12 employees servicing approximately 4,000
                      accounts.
                   -- Audit collection follow-up to determine whether proper form
                      letters are being sent and adequate investigation made.
                   -- Spot check dictated collection letters to maintain a high
                      quality with regard to wording and tie-in.
                   -- Interpret computer read-outs regarding total dollar amounts
                      in 5, 4, and 3 month delinquent accounts.
                   -- Monitor telephone collectors to determine whether they
                      follow Company policy in their basic approach and whether
                      their collection effort is adequate.
                   -- Establish collection objectives for subordinates.
                   -- Prepare wage and performance reviews on subordinates.
                   -- Interview and hire job applicants.

                   Achievements:
                   -- Substantially reduced credit losses by establishing a new
                      procedure now widely used in the Company; easily identify-
                      ing the more serious delinquent accounts, maintaining
                      tighter control over them, avoiding lost opportunities.

46

(1981-1983)   Position: Live Account Credit Supervisor

Responsibilities:
-- Handle orders rejected by the computer on balances of
   $510 and over with view toward upgrading.
-- Supervise 4 to 6 credit clerks who handle add-on orders
   on balances up to $510; personally handle correspondence
   on balances of $510 and over.
-- Review, approve or reject new customer credit applications.
-- Operate CRT station to retain up-to-date computer read-
   out regarding details of customers' accounts.

(1969-1970)   Position: Telephone Collector

Responsibilities: Contact delinquent customers by phone.

(1966-1969)   Position: Collection Manager

Responsibilities:
-- Make collection follow-up on approximately 600 accounts.
-- Determine proper form letter to fit the situation; dic-
   tate letters on situations not covered by form letters.
-- Investigate, when necessary, to obtain new information.
-- Handle any special customer correspondence required.

PERSONAL   Birthdate: 2-5-37   Single

SALARY   Open to discussion, depending on position and potential.

TRAVEL   Agreeable to any moderate amount of travel required.

LOCATE   Will consider possible relocation.

AVAILABILITY   One month's notice required.

EMPLOYER   Present employer is not aware of decision to consider change
CONTACT   and may not be contacted at this time.

REFERENCES   References available upon request.

INTERESTS   Music, theatre, reading, travel, sports.

ANDREW POPE

4712 West Highway 17
Des Moines, IA 47181
Phone: (431) 937-5843

OBJECTIVE   Superintendent of Construction

    -- 30 years of experience in all phases of construction work;
    hospitals, schools, airport terminals, power plants, high
    rise buildings, factories.

EXPERIENCE
1966 to
Present   JOHN W. MATTHEWS & CO., Des Moines, Iowa
    D. CARLSON CONSTRUCTION COMPANY, South Holland, Illinois
    EDWARD BILLS CONSTRUCTION COMPANY, Chicago, Illinois
    FRED RAGLUND & SONS, Chicago, Illinois

Positions: Superintendent
          Assistant Superintendent

Responsibilities as Superintendent: Complete charge of projects, supervising as many as 110 men -- technical, skilled
and unskilled. Work closely with sub-contractors and vendors;
approve their work and materials. Submit progress and other
reports to management, as well as recommendations on jobs.

Responsibilities as Assistant Superintendent: Assisted in the
general supervision of each project. Coordinated the activities of sub-contractors. Reviewed shop drawings and interpreted them to the men whenever necessary. Expedited delivery
of material and handled the distribution. Made up progress
reports and kept the Superintendent apprised of any problems.

Achievements:
 -- Credited for completing projects as scheduled or in less
   than scheduled time.
 -- Made suggestions to architects and other technical personnel regarding changes which were accepted and proved to
   be effective.
 -- Frequently consulted by sub-contractors and management.

Major Projects Supervised:
    Northern University, West Des Moines, Iowa
    Joliet Junior College
    Homewood-Flossmoor High School
    Six-story Community Hospital - $5 million
    Steel Mills
    A Power House, South Route Expressway
    Concourse Building at International Airport
    Addition to Granton Hospital - $4 million

1957
1966

RAGNAR BENSON, Chicago, Illinois
AUSTIN COMPANY
JAMES MC HUGH CONSTRUCTION COMPANY
INLAND CONSTRUCTION COMPANY

Position: Construction Engineer

Responsibilities: Assigned to handle all layout work, planning work schedules, ordering material, and reviewing blueprints. Supervised 3 men and worked closely with them to set up layout prior to and during construction.

In early years of experience, as a member of a survey team, worked as an Instrument Man and Rodman; achieved steady advancement, learned all phases of layout and construction work, and acquired a broad knowledge of all types of material.

PERSONAL

Born in 1937   Married
5'10"   200 Lbs.   Excellent Health

EDUCATION

Chicago Technical College
   Courses: Drafting; Blue Print Reading

ACTIVITIES

Participate in many sports. Past member of a Technical Association.

BRETT R. WILSON

2938 Center Drive
Burnside, WI 62941
Telephone: (414) 325-6167

OBJECTIVE   <u>Controller or Assistant Controller</u>

SUMMARY   A well qualified, profit-oriented Management Executive whose
              accounting and controllership capabilities have been demon-
              strated by successful experience.

AREAS OF   Controllership   Budgets, Forecasts
KNOWLEDGE   Audits
              Accounting Administration   Payroll
              Financial Accounting
              Industrial Accounting   Departmental Supervision
              Cost Accounting   Management Liaison
              Accounting Systems   Data Processing Usage

              Consolidations   Employment, Training

PERSONAL   Birthdate: 9-13-41   Married, Two children
              6'   185 Lbs.   Excellent Health

EDUCATION   Northwestern University, Chicago, Illinois
                 B.B.A. Degree
                 Major: Business Administration
              University of Chicago, Chicago, Illinois
                 CPA Review course and various Seminars

PROFESSIONAL
MEMBERSHIP   National Association of Accountants

EXPERIENCE
1979 to   MAREMONT, INC., Milwaukee, WI
Present   Conglomerate corporation; manufacturing, mining, agricultural,
              building and hardware. Annual volume $200 million.

              <u>Position</u>: Manager of Corporate Accounting
                        Acting Controller - England
                        Acting Controller - Canada

              <u>Responsibilities</u>:
              -- Develop, implement and manage corporate accounting, which
                 includes consolidated statements of 19 Divisions.
              -- Prepare budgets, and act in the capacity of Assistant Cor-
                 porate Controller.

50

Achievements:
-- Made major savings in time and expense by standardizing the annual audit.
-- As Acting Controller for England and Canada, effected numerous changes to get these Divisions out of trouble.
-- On special assignments to Erie and Detroit, installed systems improvements which saved the Division $75,000; prepared a Divisional budget.
-- Established the accounting format of a newly purchased Division.

1976
1979

GREGGHAND CORPORATION, Chicago, Illinois.
Conglomerate corporation; transportation, computer leasing, industrial chemicals, food services.

Position: Staff Accountant

Responsibilities:
-- Review companies' financial statements and write status reports.
-- Review for approval all authority for expenditure for the Controller.
-- Study Divisional cost statements for possible improvements.
-- Prepare annual forecast for Chicago Office.
-- Submit reports to NYSE and I.C.C.
-- Special assignments: audits, annual report design, new accounting presentation.

Achievements:
-- Designed effective new corporate financial statements which presented more facts to management and permitted better decision making.
-- Reduced reporting time from 12th working day to 7th working day.

1974
1976

APEX SMELTING, Division of American Metal Climax, Chicago, Illinois. Manufacturers of aluminum alloys; 4 Plants. Division annual volume $25 million.

Position: Staff Accountant to the Controller

Responsibilities:
-- Prepare consolidated statements, annual profit plan, long range plan and statement analysis.
-- Assist in developing cost data for computer program.
-- Coordinate new inventory system with IBM.
-- Assist in preparation of capital budget; establish uniform system of fixed assets.
-- Responsible for function of Accounting Department.

Achievements:

-- Assisted Controller in establishing financial headquarters in Chicago; consolidated all accounting operations for the 4 plants.
-- Established uniform NCR system, statements, chart of accounts and other procedures for 4 plants.

1972
1974

ASBESTOS AND MAGNESIA COMPANY, Chicago, Illinois
Leading distributor of insulation materials.

Position: Chief Accountant

Responsibilities:

-- Direct and manage the complete operation of the office staff of 25.
-- Handle general ledger, accounts payable, accounts receivable, office and field payrolls; prepare union and tax returns involving 4 states.
-- Prepare financial statements, handle perpetual inventory system, operate the credit and group hospitalization program.
-- Recruit, screen, hire and train employees.

SALARY

Open to discussion depending on position, potential and location.

TRAVEL

Agreeable to the amount required by the position.

LOCATE

Readily willing to relocate, including foreign assignments.

AVAILABILITY

3-4 weeks' notice required.

EMPLOYER
CONTACT

Present employer is not aware of decision to consider change and may not be contacted at this time.

REFERENCES

References available upon request.

CHARLES W. WEBER

4942 North Milland
St. Louis, MO 38192
Telephone: (314) 588-4188

OBJECTIVE   Credit Management

AREAS OF   Credit Management   Direct Loans
KNOWLEDGE   Departmental Administration   Industrial Leases
AND   Industrial Credit and   Conditional Sales Contracts
EXPERIENCE   Collection   Security Agreements
                 Consumer Credit and
                     Collection   Collection Agencies
                                                  Document Preparation
                 Credit Investigation   Insurance Verification
                 Accounts Receivable
                 Financial Statement Analysis   Management Reports
                                                  Staff Supervision
                 Dealer-Distributor Relations
                 Nationwide Accounts

PERSONAL   Birthdate: 12-12-50   Married, One child
                 6'   190 Lbs.   Excellent Health

EDUCATION   Washington University, St. Louis, MO - 3 years
                     Major: Business Administration

EXPERIENCE
July, 1981   AAA INDUSTRIAL CREDIT COMPANY, Northfield, Missouri
Nov., 1986   Industrial leasing and financing. $29 million outstandings.

                 Position: Credit Manager

                 Responsibilities:
                  -- Maintain full credit responsibility for 680 national ac-
                     counts.
                  -- Manage and direct all collection activities.
                  -- Direct the credit extension to customers; analyze the ori-
                     ginal proposals; analyze financial statements; make credit
                     investigations; establish limits.
                  -- Maintain personal liaison with collection agencies and at-
                     torneys.
                  -- Prepare all required documentation.
                  -- Manage the office; act for the Regional Manager in his ab-
                     sence.
                  -- Prepare periodic management statistical reports for the
                     corporate home office.
                  -- Supervise 2 staff employees.

Achievements:
-- Successfully maintained past due accounts under 3%.
-- Kept all losses below the projected percentage of sales.

Aug., 1976
Apr., 1981

TEXACO, INC., Chicago, Illinois

Position: Credit Man

Responsibilities:
-- Full personal authority on credit, collections and customer service on 65,000 active accounts located throughout
   the United States.
-- Direct the handling of commercial accounts, fraud accounts, unauthorized charges and skip tracing.
-- Manage and control all activities in connection with delinquent accounts.
-- Supervise, train and motivate a group of 8 employees
   handling the assigned accounts.

Dec., 1975
Aug., 1976

AUTOMATIC ELECTRIC COMPANY, Northlake, Illinois
Equipment manufacturer for General Telephone Company.

Position: Buyer

Responsibilities:
-- Purchase plant supplies, including all items necessary for
   plant operations, except raw materials and components.

Reason for Change: Resigned to begin a career in the credit
field.

SALARY   Open to discussion in general range of current earnings.

TRAVEL   Agreeable to amount required for the position -- up to 40%

LOCATE   Willing to relocate.

AVAILABILITY   Immediate

EMPLOYER   Past employers may be contacted at any time
CONTACT

MILITARY   U.S. Army. 1973-1975. Honorable Discharge

DEBRA GOODYEAR

639 Park Place
Kansas City, MO 38321
Telephone: (818) 324-4934

OBJECTIVE Customer Relations Manager/Administrative Ma

AREAS OF Administration   Customer S
KNOWLEDGE Long Range Planning   Service Ma
    Profit and Loss Statements Service Tr
    Department Administration Customer Sales/Orders
    Budget Planning, Control Handling Complaints
    Computer Programs   Liaison with Customers
    Management by Objectives
    Liaison with Regional Managers Personnel
    Liaison with Dept. Managers Employee Training, Counseling
    Liaison with Manufacturers Employee Benefits Administra-
     Representatives   tion
             Turnover Control

PERSONAL Birthdate: 10-3-45   Widow, Two children
    5'5" 125 Lbs.

EDUCATION Georgia State College, Atlanta - 2 years
    Emory University, Atlanta - 1-1/2 years
     Major: Education Minor: Languages

    Special Training:
     Loyola University, Los Angeles - 1 year
      Business Management
     U.C.L.A., Los Angeles - Accounting

PROFESSIONAL American Management Association: former member
MEMBERSHIPS, National Management Association
ACTIVITIES Kansas City Women's Traffic Club
    Midwest International Air Cargo Association: Board of Directors
    International Trade Club of Missouri
    Business and Professional Women's Club

EXPERIENCE
Nov., 1980 THE FLYING TIGER LINE, INC.
to Present World's largest air freight airline.

(Feb., 1982 Position: Regional Manager of Customer Service - Midwest
to Present)

Responsibilities:
-- Plan, control, direct and coordinate all Company customer
   service activities in Midwest Region; 16 state area.
-- Plan and control yearly budget; customer service - $350,000;
   communications - $150,000; public relations - $15,000.
-- Coordinate Regional customer service activities with other
   customer service groups within the Company, domestic and
   international
-- Maintain close liaison with Sales, Marketing and Operations
   Departments within the Region.
-- Provide senior management with reports and statistics.
-- Train and develop customer service personnel; administer em-
   ployee benefits.

Achievements:
-- Successfully implemented first (and only) regionalized customer service and communications unit, giving customers in the
   16 state region greatly expanded service (24 hours per day,
   365 days per year), at a cost reduction of 30.6%
-- Company now considered to be Number One in the industry for
   customer service in the Midwest.
-- Implemented changes in the communications system which reduced costs by 18% and increased overall effectiveness.
-- Planned and coordinated first regional public relations campaign; produced a 27% increase in awareness factor of the
   company in the Midwest.
-- Planned and implemented Directory Reference System in the
   computer -- now used by all Customer Service offices in
   system.
-- Developed and implemented first telephone sales program
   within Customer Service; now standard operating practice in
   the Midwest Region.
-- Developed 4 people who moved up to supervisory/management
   positions both within and outside of Region.
-- First woman line manager in Company's history.

(Nov., 1980   Position: Supervisor Customer Service Training and Sales Adminis-
Feb., 1982)   tration

Responsibilities:
-- Determine the training needs of customer service supervisors
   and representatives.
-- Develop, implement and coordinate customer service training
   programs throughout the domestic system, including techniques
   of supervision, service and telephone sales.

56

Achievements:
-- Planned and coordinated first systemwide meeting of customer service managers and supervisors; result was standardization of procedures throughout the system.
-- Implemented new and improved training methods and techniques; developed a training procedures manual.

(Oct., 1978
Nov., 1980)

THE ATLANTIC AIRLINE SCHOOL OF CALIFORNIA, Inglewood, California

Position: Senior Instructor

(1964
1977)

DELTA AIR LINES

Positions and Responsibilities:

(1975-1977)	Atlanta	Airport Ticket Center, Downtown Offices, Ticket Mail Center.
(1971-1975)	Los Angeles	Downtown Offices; Acting Chief Agent for 5 city ticket offices.
(1964-1971)	Atlanta	Downtown Ticket Offices Airline Ticket Counter Secretary to Internal Auditor

SALARY — Open to discussion; responsibilities and challenge are important.

TRAVEL — Agreeable to any amount required to do the job well; current position requires extensive travel, both domestic and overseas.

LOCATE — Readily willing to relocate.

AVAILABILITY — Prefer to give 30 days' notice.

EMPLOYER CONTACT — Present employer is not aware of decision to change and may not be contacted at this time.

REFERENCES — References are available upon request.

INTERESTS — Golf, swimming, reading, painting.

FOREIGN LANGUAGE — Spanish: read, write, speak

DAVID M. CARSON

2918 Wood Lane
LaGrange, IL 60525
Telephone: (312) 588-5315

OBJECTIVE   Corporate Creative Design Management

AREAS OF   As Designer:
KNOWLEDGE AND   Exhibits, Displays, Film and TV Commercials
EXPERIENCE   Interior-Exterior Logos and Graphics
                       Presentation Drawings and Illustrations
                       Machine and Structural Working Drawings

                   As Artisan:
                       All Media of Painting Execution
                       Stat, Hot Press and Color Key Operations
                       Photo and Cut Silk Screen Methods
                       Fiberglass, Plexiglass, Urethane Foam
                       Polyester Casting and Laminating Resins
                       Portrait and Landscape Artist, Muralist, Teacher

                   As Manager:
                       Time and Material Estimates
                       Material Procurement
                       Job and Manpower Scheduling
                       Shop and Location Supervision

PROFESSIONAL   Certified: Professional Design Director, Set Designer, and Scenic
CERTIFICATION   Artist, by United Scenic Artists of America
                   Certified: To teach all levels of Art by the State of Illinois

EDUCATION   Southern Illinois University, Carbondale, Illinois 1970-1975
                       B.A. Degree - 1975
                           Major: Art Education   Minor: Fine Art
                       Associate Degree in Commercial Art - 1972

EMPLOYER   Present employer is not aware of decision to consider change and
CONTACT   may not be contacted at this time.

EXPERIENCE

1968 to
Present

AMERICAN BROADCASTING COMPANY, Chicago, Illinois
Nationwide television broadcasting.

Position: Set Designer

Responsibilities:
-- Coordinate and develop the design of all off and on-air set
   presentations of ABC-TV, Chicago area (Sales and Programming).
-- Prepare presentation roughs and comprehensive drawings.
-- Plan and direct the execution of all carpenter drawings,
   painting elevations, and studio or location drawings.
-- Manage the activities of 18 employees on 2 shifts; add or re-
   lease manpower as per job requirements.

1981 to
Present
(Concurrent)

AMERICAN SCENE, Chicago, Illinois
Contractor-subcontractor for design and execution of commercial
display, industrial theatrical graphics and scenery.

Position: Manager, Designer, Artist

Responsibilities:
-- Synthesize client needs into conceptual design.
-- Render presentation drawings; prepare working drawings.
-- Execute painting.
-- If local, supervise installation.
-- Provide general management to the business; profit responsi-
   bility, supervision, client contact.

Designed and Executed:
..IBM Show, Hawaii
..American Bankers Association Show, San Francisco
..International Harvester Show, Pick Congress, Chicago
..Recreational Home Show, McCormick Place, Chicago
..IBM Show, Acapulco, Mexico

1970-
1977

ST. LOUIS MUNICIPAL OPERA
Largest opera company in the Midwest; annual budget $8 million.

Position: Scenic Artist

Responsibilities:
-- Scale, paint and execute dimensional landscapes, interiors
   and exteriors on flat muslin up to 40' high x 150' wide.

Achievements:
-- Started as apprentice and achieved distinction of being the
   best scenic artist at the opera.
-- Painted scenes for over 70 operas and plays.

59

CYRUS E. BALL, F.I.D.S.A.

1130 South Indiana Avenue
Indianapolis, IN 51241
Telephone: (317) 427-3235

OBJECTIVE   Industrial Design/Product Development

AREAS OF   Cook and Bake Ware   Electric Housewares
KNOWLEDGE   Plastic Ware, Wire Goods   Coffee and Tea Makers
                                             Can Openers, Gadgets
                 Premium Products
                 Power Tools   Kitchen Tools
                 Illustration, Graphics   Cutlery, Flatware

PROFESSIONAL   Fellow, Industrial Designers Society of America
MEMBERSHIPS,   Past Chairman, Midwest Chapter
ACTIVITIES   Past Midwest Regional Vice President
                 Listed in "Who's Who in the Midwest" and "Who's Who in American
                     Art"
                 Work represented in International Design Annuals

EXPERIENCE
1980   INTERCRAFT INDUSTRIES CORPORATION, Indianapolis, IN
to Present   Manufacturer of wall decorations and photo frames.

                 Position: Senior Designer, New Product Development

                 Responsibilities:
                 -- To consult with top and middle management on problems in-
                    volving new products.
                 -- To create marketable products within the Company's merchan-
                    dising goals and cost structure.
                 -- To design three dimensional products within the Company's
                    full product range.
                 -- To design two and three dimensional art to be sold as wall
                    decorations.
                 -- To work with model shop, silk screen department and tool room
                    on the preparation of prototypes for market testing; display
                    samples of newly developed products for trade shows.

60

Achievements:
-- Designed a number of plastic frames which became basic, high
   sales items.
-- Designed several lines of silk screened pictures which were
   successful in the framed art market.
-- Designed many graphic pieces to stimulate sales of photo and
   documentary frames.
-- Designed line of three dimensional wall decorations, successful in the market place.

1978-
1980

BANKO MANGO DESIGN ASSOCIATES, INC., Chicago, Illinois.

Position: Senior Designer and Account Manager

Responsibilities:
-- To consult with clients to determine parameters of design
   projects; record the limits, general purposes, merchandising
   goals, cost factors and other pertinent data.
-- To prepare estimated time/cost quotations for the job.
-- To solicit new clients for the Company.
-- To design products, and contact sub-contractors and sup-
   pliers.
-- To work with client's manufacturing engineers where re-
   quired.

Achievements:
-- Handled or was involved in design of products for Sears Roe-
   buck and Co., including items such as: portable electric
   tools, bench grinders, bench saws, radial arm saws, hand
   tools, lawn sprinklers, pruners.
-- Successfully designed products for manufacturers of bath accessories, shower stalls, floor mops and plastic items.

1973-
1978

KNAPP DESIGN ASSOCIATES, INC., River Forest, Illinois

Position: Director of Design Administration and Associate

Responsibilities:
-- To meet with clients and determine all general and specific
   aspects of a design job, and make quotations.
-- To schedule design jobs through the organization.
-- To work with model shop on preparation of prototypes.
-- To supervise junior design personnel.

Achievements:
-- Designed a line of enameled cast aluminum for Club Aluminum
   Company which won a design award from the National House-
   wares Manufacturers Association.
-- Designed a highly successful console for a computerized type
   composing unit.
-- Designed a tachistoscopic device used for speed reading; ac-
   quired a very sound mechanical patent on the unit.

| 1971– | PLASTIC TOOLING AIDS LABORATORY, Bridgeport, Connecticut. |
| 1973 | Consultants on plastic molding problems and molding of injection molded plastic prototypes. |

Position: Manager, Midwest Division (Skokie, Illinois)

Responsibilities:
-- Full personal responsibility for the Midwest facility, including client contact, sales and promotion.
-- To program the sequence of work through the shop, and maintain quality control.
-- To prepare quotations, consolidate costs and prepare invoices.

Achievements:
-- Assisted many corporations in solving unusual molding problems involving newly developed plastics; Teletype Corporation, Toastmaster Division McGraw Edison, Hotpoint.

| 1964– | EKCO PRODUCTS COMPANY, Chicago, Illinois. Major housewares manu- |
| 1971 | facturer. Sales volume over $100 million. |

Position: Corporate Director of Design

Responsibilities:
-- To direct staff designers and the model shop, with a basic function to delineate the appearance and use/function design of new products and lines, and improve existing products.
-- To provide design service, from sketches to prototypes, to Product Managers.
-- To coordinate design, function, materials and processes for new and improved processes.
-- To maintain liaison with top level corporate officers.

Achievements:
-- Over 150 U.S. and foreign patents granted on design and mechanical solutions to projects.
-- Numerous designs still have market acceptance 20 years after conception.

SALARY   Negotiable in range of current earnings, depending on potential.

LOCATE   Readily willing to relocate.

AVAILABILITY   Immediate.

DAVID B. ROWLAND

2118 North Echo Lane
Wheaton, IL 60038
Telephone: (312) 335-0854

OBJECTIVE   Distribution Center Manager
                              or
                     National Distribution Manager

AREAS OF   Distribution Center Management   Budget Preparation, Control
KNOWLEDGE   Material Handling, Storage   Expense Control
                     Receiving, Shipping   Cost Analysis

                     Traffic Management   Office Management
                     Transportation Patterns
                     Rail, Common Carriers,   New Warehouse: Planning and
                        Leased Trucks   Opening
                     Loss and Damage Claims   Warehouse Layout

                     Automated Order Filling   Computer Usage
                     Mail Order Handling   Systems and Procedures
                                                       Personnel Supervision
                     Computerized Inventory Control   Wage Administration, Surveys

PERSONAL   Birthdate: 12-23-45   Married, Family
                     6'2"   225 Lbs.   Good health

EDUCATION   Texas Christian University, Ft. Worth, Texas
                     Rutgers University, New Brunswick, New Jersey
                        80 Credit Hours in Evening Divisions
                        Major: Accounting   Minor: Traffic Management

EXPERIENCE
1963 to   LARGE FINISHED GOODS DISTRIBUTING COMPANY
Present

(August, 1982   Position: Distribution Center Manager - Chicago
to Present)
                     Responsibilities:
                     -- Full personal responsibility for the management of the Chi-
                        cago Distribution Center: $60 million annual volume, 300,000
                        square feet; 85 employees; operating budget of $1.1 million.
                     -- Major responsibilities: (1) control expenses; (2) provide
                        quality service to stores and customers.
                     -- Supervise operations of the Center, involving these areas:
                        inventory control, order filling, receiving and shipping,
                        traffic, leased trucks, accounts receivable, accounts pay-
                        able, consumer mail orders, security, maintenance, personnel
                        and employee morale.

63

Achievements:
-- Chicago Warehouse ranked 7th out of 9 in the U.S. in 1980 -- now ranked 2nd.
-- In 1983, volume of merchandise handled increased 6.5%; expenses were decreased by 10%.
-- Saved $20,000 per year by contracting for disposal of waste.
-- Reduced labor force from about 120 in 1980 to 76 in January, 1984, while maintaining approximately the same volume.
-- Reduced the audit shortage from $90,000 to under $8,000 per year.

(1980-1982)   Position: Assistant Distribution Center Manager - Chicago.

Responsibilities:
-- Controlled the daily operations of the Chicago Warehouse, production and clerical.
-- Planned the production manpower needs for volume to be handled.
-- Scheduled and coordinated the various departments to provide for an efficient operation.
-- Opened the Atlanta Distribution Center on a special 3-month assignment.

(1978-1980)   Position: Assistant Distribution Center Manager, Fort Worth, TX

Responsibilities:
-- Overall management of the day-to-day operation of this Regional Warehouse of 240,000 square feet with 60 employees.

(1975-1978)   Position: Assistant Distribution Center Manager, Metuchen, N.J.

Responsibilities:
-- Responsibilities similar to those in directing daily operations in Fort worth and Chicago Warehouses; 250,000 square feet with 70 employees.
-- Special assignment of 30 days to open the Chicago Center.

(1973-1975)   Positions: Various assignments at the Fort Worth Warehouse, including line foreman in charge of order filling, stoc control and receiving.

EMPLOYER   Present employer is not aware of decision to consider change and
CONTACT   should not be contacted.

DR. DAVID S. WYETH

287 North Dixon Street
Haddon Heights, NJ 02177
Telephone: (212) 406-2199

OBJECTIVE   Vice President and Economist

AREAS OF   Business Forecasting   Econometrics
KNOWLEDGE AND   Corporate Planning and   Statistics
EXPERIENCE   Development   Balance-of-Payments Analysis
                    Financial Analysis   Management Consulting
                    Management Science   Data Processing - Computers
                    Marketing Research

EDUCATION   Post Doctorate, 1970-1972, Purdue University, W. LaFayette, IN
                    Ph.D. Degree, 1968, Cornell University, Ithaca, New York
                    M.S. Degree, 1964, Cornell University, Ithaca, New York

PROFESSIONAL   National Association of Business Economists -- President, Jersey
STATUS AND   Economic Club Chapter
MEMBERSHIPS   Economics Committee of the Grocery Manufacturers Association
                    Balance-of-Payments Committee, The Nat'l. Foreign Trade Council
                    American Statistical Association -- President, Local Chapter
                    Mid-west Economic Association
                    American Economic Association -- Steering Committee member,
                        Caucus of Black Economists
                    National Committee on Rural Affairs and Agri-business, U.S.
                        Chamber of Commerce
                    Advisory Boards of (a) the University of New Jersey Technical
                        College and (b) Atlanta University Graduate School of Busi-
                        ness.
                    Policy Board, The Ford Foundation - sponsored Black Economists
                        Development Project

EXPERIENCE
1975 to   LEADING FOOD CONGLOMERATE, Metuchen, NJ
Present
                    Position: Corporate Economist
                              Visiting Lecturer in Quantitative Analysis, University
                              of New Jersey Graduate School of Business

                    Responsibilities:
                     -- Economic advisory services to top corporate executives, indi-
                        vidually and collectively.
                     -- Business forecasting for planning, financing, investment and
                        hedging of risk purposes.
                     -- Business research/analysis for corporate portfolio.

-- Economic briefings to divisional managers on an on-going basis.
-- Consulting services on request to other corporate functions; procurement, transportation, commercial research, international, business models and time-sharing computer applications.

Achievements:
-- Established the Office of Corporate Economics and worked as Chief Economist of the Executive Office.
-- Major responsibility in engineering the technical base underlying what has been judged to be among the top 10 corporate planning and development systems for U.S. corporations.
-- Conducted the economic and strategic research that underpegged the successful major corporate acquisition efforts.
-- Represented the corporation's interest on numerous national committees and trade associations.
-- Contributed to the corporate image through extensive lectures and public appearances on economic topics.

Reason for Considering Change: To seek new challenges and opportunities for professional advancement.

1973-1975   HOWARD UNIVERSITY, Washington, D.C.

Position: Associate Professor of Economics and Statistics
          Consultant to the Computer Laboratory

Responsibilities:
-- Conducted graduate courses in managerial economics, statistics, and operations research.
-- As professor, supervised graduate students' programs, theses preparation, and progress toward graduate degrees.
-- As consultant to the Computer Laboratory, conducted seminars on use of computers and consulted with individual researchers on statistical design for analysis of projects.
-- Lectured widely at off-campus conferences and meetings.
-- Served as Consulting Economist to several regional and national businesses as well as non-profit organizations.

1971-1973   TURNERS GLASS WORKS, Ithaca, New York

Position: Senior Statistician and Operations Research Scientist

Responsibilities:
-- Aided in introducing statistical technique of design of experiment and scientific computers into the corporate R & D function.
-- Team member and consulting statistician on all on-going projects of the Process Research Center.
-- Weekly visits to various locations to offer "open-house" consulting services to Company-wide researchers and scientists.

-- Aided in the decisions and implementations of the Company's first Data Logging System.
-- Consulting Statistician to Company's quality control and reliability functions.

1970-1971   PURDUE UNIVERSITY, West LaFayette, Indiana.

Position: Post-Doctoral Fellow and Visiting Scholar.

Responsibilities:
-- Conducted research on economics of technological change and aided in the supervision of students' programs, theses preparation, and progress toward Ph.D. status.
-- Collaborated with professors in econometrics, statistics, computer science and management science in order to deepen personal knowledge level in these previously studied fields.
-- Consulting Economist to several companies.
-- Participated in the Quantitative Industrial Management Seminar of the Institute of Quantitative Management.

1968-1970   NORTH DAKOTA STATE UNIVERSITY, Bismark, North Dakota

Position: Assistant Professor of Economics and Statistics; Staff Economist, North Dakota Agricultural Experiment Station

Responsibilities:
-- Taught undergraduate and graduate courses in economics, linear programming, statistics and econometrics; supervised graduate students' theses preparation.
-- Consulting economist to companies and government agencies.
-- Member of technical committees coordinating and conducting regional research for the North Central and Great Plains States.

EMPLOYER   Present employer is not aware of decision to consider change and
CONTACT   may not be contacted at this time.

REFERENCES   References available immediately upon request.

DOUGLAS TAYLOR, Ph.D.

2310 Jericho Avenue
DeKalb, IL 60112
Telephone: (313) 457-2308

OBJECTIVE   <u>Department Chairman</u>
                -- Animal Science

AREAS OF   Animal Science   Project Development
KNOWLEDGE   Animal Nutrition   Appropriations and Funding

AREAS OF KNOWLEDGE	
Animal Science	Project Development
Animal Nutrition	Appropriations and Funding
Poultry	Public Relations
Physiology	Government Relations
Breeding	
Feeds and Feeding	Accounting
	Business Administration
Teaching	Budget Control
Counseling	
	Agriculture
Research	Home Economics
Computer Applications	Technology
	Chemistry
Academic Program Development	
Seminars	Psychology
Associations	

EDUCATION   Universities - University of Illinois, Purdue, Southern Illinois
               Degrees - B.S., Agriculture, University of Illinois
                       M.S., Agriculture, Purdue University
                       Ph.D., Animal Science, University of Illinois

MEMBERSHIPS American Association of Animal Science
            American Association for Advancement of Science
            World Poultry Science Association
            American Institute of Biological Science

CITATION   "American Men of Science," listed.
LISTINGS   "Leaders in American Science," listed.
            "Who's Who in American Education," listed.

EXPERIENCE
1965 to
Present

NORTHERN ILLINOIS UNIVERSITY, DeKalb, IL (28,000 students).

Positions: Professor of Animal Industries, following promotions
from:
Associate Professor of Animal Industries
Assistant Professor of Animal Industries

1976 to
Present

As Professor of Animal Industries:

Responsibilities and Achievements:
-- Conducted successful graduate courses in Animal Nutrition,
Poultry Nutrition, Seminar, Advanced Readings, and Individual Research.
-- Directed productive graduate research in Poultry Nutrition,
Physiology, and Products, and in related specialized areas.
-- As a member of the Graduate Council, representing the Schools
of Agriculture, Home Economics, and Technology, evaluated
and approved new graduate programs of study proposed by the
different schools and departments of this multi-campus university.
-- As a member of the School of Agriculture made effective contributions in Committees for Agriculture Research Facilities,
Seminars, and Rank and Promotion.
-- As major professor successfully supervised graduate students'
programs, theses preparation, and progress toward Ph.D.
status.
-- Published 10 research papers in collaboration with graduate
students and staff members.
-- In questionnaire ratings by students, earned "Above Average"
rating in 63% of the returns and "Excellent" rating in 18%.
-- As member of the United States Participation Team at World
Poultry Congress in Kiev, Russia, broadened scope of professional knowledge by observations in Russia, and subsequently
in Germany, France, Yugoslavia, Romania, and Sweden.

1968-1976

As Associate Professor of Animal Industries:

Responsibilities and Achievements:
-- Organized and directed graduate student research programs
through Cooperative Research Grants from Illinois Department
of Agriculture.
-- Designed and accomplished the implementation of Masters Degree Programs in Animal Industries.
-- Wrote and published a State Agricultural Bulletin, as well as
33 papers in other technical publications.
-- Received national award recognition for contributions to
poultry and egg industry.
-- As Chief Academic Advisor substantially improved Agricultural
Counseling by accomplishing a more direct contact between
students and faculty.

1965-1968	As Assistant Professor of Animal Industries:

1965-1968   As Assistant Professor of Animal Industries:

-- As Chairman of School of Agriculture Public Relations Committee was materially instrumental in obtaining a $2,000,000 appropriation from the Illinois State Legislature for new Agricultural Building.

-- Organized the establishment of new classroom and laboratory facilities for the department, in the new building.

-- On leave (1965-1967) completed work and received Doctorate Degree in Animal Science from the University of Illinois.

-- Published 9 papers and articles in technical journals.

1961-1965   Instructor -- School of Vocations and Professions, S.I.U.

1954-1961   Manager -- Commercial Poultry Farm

1952-1954   Executive Secretary -- Indiana State Poultry Association.

TRAVEL   Agreeable to any travel requirement normally associated with this position.

LOCATE   Readily willing to relocate.

AVAILABILITY   Within two months after hiring arrangement.

EMPLOYER CONTACT   Present employer should not be contacted except by mutual arrangement following provisional commitment to hire.

REFERENCES   Excellent professional and personal references are available immediately upon request.

JULIO MARTINEZ

1812 Washington Street
Des Plaines, IL 60015
Telephone: (312) 848-7322

OBJECTIVE

Civil Engineering
-- Design or Construction Supervision

AREAS OF
KNOWLEDGE AND
EXPERIENCE

Civil Engineering

Design Engineering

Rural Freeway Design
Right of Way Design
Hydraulic and Hydrologic
    Design
Drainage System Design

Retaining Wall Design
Reinforced Box Culvert Design

Drafting

Cost Estimates
Specifications Development

Construction Supervision
Field Surveys
Field Supervision

Preliminary Bridge (Site) Report
CPM Charts Checking

Mathematics (Pure and Applied)

EDUCATION

St. Martin's College, Olympia, Washington
    1963-1966
        Major: Civil Engineering   Minor: Mathematics
University of New Mexico, Albuquerque, New Mexico
    B.S. Degree - 1969
        Major: Mathematics
DePaul University, Chicago
    M.S. in Mathematics - 1975
Special Training: Illinois Institute of Technology
    Engineering refresher courses for professional engineers.

PROFESSIONAL
MEMBERSHIP,
CERTIFICATION

Illinois Association of Highway Engineers: Member
Professional Engineer Registration: State of Illinois

71

WORK EXPERIENCE

1969-1985   DEPARTMENT OF TRANSPORTATION, STATE OF ILLINOIS, 595 South
                State Street, Elgin, Illinois

                Position: Civil Engineer II

                Design Responsibilities:
                -- Rural and urban highway projects.
                -- Drainage systems.
                -- Retaining walls and reinforced concrete box culverts.
                -- Supervision of draftsmen; personal drafting in special
                   situations.
                -- Field surveys for preliminary topographical, cross-sectional
                   and right of way works.

                Construction Responsibilities:
                -- Layout and inspection of highways, bridges and drainage
                   systems.
                -- Calculation of earthworks, pavement areas and all other pay
                   quantities.
                -- Progress reports, inspection reports and documentation.

                Achievements:
                -- As a member of design team, played a vital role in the suc-
                   cessful design of various projects within time and cost
                   limitations.
                -- Maximum utilization of EDP facilities and mathematical compu-
                   tation permitted engineering costs to be minimized.
                -- As an Assistant Resident Engineer and Resident Engineer on an
                   interstate highway project (I-90), which included a $4.3 mil-
                   lion interchange, successfully maintained construction pro-
                   gress on schedule and within limits of planned engineering
                   costs; total engineering costs only 95% of budget.
                -- Effectively implemented erosion control measures on side
                   slopes and ditches at the project.

                Reason for Change: State government budget reduction for economy.

Nov., 1985   MACE ASSOCIATES, 85 East Wacker Drive, Chicago, Ill. 60601.
to Present   Planners, architects and consulting engineers.

                Position: Highway Design Engineer

                Responsibilities:
                -- Design of rural expressway highway.
                -- Hydrological and drainage calculation on highway and bridge
                   project.
                -- Design and drafting of typical sections of highways.
                -- Checking and calculating of vertical curves.
                -- Consulting for various problems on the project.

                                    72

EDGAR R. MITCHELL

1621 Central Avenue
Baltimore, MD 08167
Telephone: (211) 322-8995

OBJECTIVE   <u>Director of Engineering</u>
                -- Plan, conduct, direct projects of major significance; apply
                   organizing and management skills toward problem solving and
                   improving engineering operations and related activities.

AREAS OF   Project Engineering   Test Equipment Design
KNOWLEDGE AND   Electro-Mechanical Systems   Instrumentation
EXPERIENCE   Mechanical Engineering   Audio Systems
                                               High Fidelity
                  Engineering Administration   Standards Laboratory De-
                  Reporting Controls   velopment

                  Department Liaison   Vendor Evaluation, Selec-
                  Staff Supervision   tion, Relations
                                               Budgeting
                  Manufacturing Engineering   Quality Control
                  Prototype Fabrication   Scheduling
                  Production Pilot Runs   Production Control

PROFESSIONAL   Institute of Electrical and Electronics Engineers
MEMBERSHIPS   Eastern Acoustical and Audio Group - Past Secretary
                  Society of American Value Engineers

EXPERIENCE
1979 to   EASTERN MANUFACTURING CORPORATION, Baltimore.
Present   Manufacturer of coin operated vending machines and phonographs.
                  Sales volume $26 million.

                  <u>Position</u>: Chief Administrative Engineer
                           Report to Vice President of Engineering

                  <u>Responsibilities:</u>
                  -- Full responsibility for all phases of engineering with the
                     exception of product design and development.
                  -- Direct a staff of 25 engineers, model makers, technicians and
                     clerical people who serve as a coordinating center between
                     two engineering groups for the company's two main product
                     areas.

73

-- Specific areas under personal control include:
Assembly of engineering prototypes; conducting life tests; material and component testing.
Development of bills of material, reproduction and distribution of engineering documents; coding of bills of material for computer input.
Preparation of drafting manual; standards and specifications for materials, parts and components.
Liaison with all operating departments.
Product approvals from Underwriters Laboratories and Canadian Standards Association.
Maintenance of all engineering documents on microfilm.

Achievements:
-- Through personnel and position evaluation, made improvements which led to greater efficiency of operations. Engineering Department services now at a much higher level in both quantity and quality, performed with fewer employees.
-- Saved $100,000 per year with standardized hardware, materials and components.
-- Instituted a value engineering program during assembly of engineering prototypes to reduce parts cost and labor; 1983 savings were $60,000.
-- Updated Department equipment and layout for greater efficiency of operation; savings of $40,000 per year.
-- Developed effective system for establishing engineering goals and budgets, thereby providing accountability and personnel responsiveness.
-- Converted manual form of bill of material to computer form.
-- Improved scheduling of engineering programs by better methods of estimating time requirements for projects.

1965-1979   HAMMOND CORPORATION, Chicago. Makers of electric organs. Annual sales $90 million.

Positions: Manager, Quality Assurance   (1977-1979)
           Manager, Product Design   (1971-1977)
           Manager, Electrical Design   (1968-1971)
           Manager, Test Department   (1965-1968)

Responsibilities:
-- As Manager, Quality Assurance, supervised a staff of 75 employees; reported to the President.
-- Reorganized the Department, developing techniques for detecting and preventing errors rather than curing defects. Functions included in-process and final audit, preparation of inspection methods, instructions for incoming inspection, engineering participation in design project teams, metrology, gage calibration control and vendor evaluation.

Achievements:

-- Developed a successful feedback system utilizing information drawn from dealers and company representatives; materially assisted Marketing and Engineering Departments to eliminate failure trends; improved product performance and reliability.
-- Established analysis procedures for returned parts.
-- Designed periodic reports used to correct design or manufacturing defects.
-- Installed effective centralized gage calibration program.
-- Wrote Quality Assurance manual and charter.
-- Developed procedure for vendor evaluation and certification.

EDUCATION

R.C.A. Institute
Illinois Institute of Technology
   3-year BSEE Program
University of Illinois
   Executive Development Program - 1977
Special Training on a Graduate Level:
   Value Analysis, Pert, C.P.M., Quality Control, Value Engineering, Technical Writing

AVAILABILITY

30 days' notice required.

EMPLOYER
CONTACT

Present employer may be contacted upon conclusion of negotiations and acceptance of position.

FRANCIS L. BAUER

10 Oak Tree
Kearney, NE 68949
Telephone: (398) 326-8953

OBJECTIVE   Manager, Industrial Engineering

HIGHLIGHTS OF
ENGINEERING/
MANAGEMENT
CAREER

For a Plastics and Chemical Manufacturer:
..Set up new I.E. Department; designed all forms and reports.
..Developed and installed manpower control system. (Savings
  $50,000 per year.)
..Developed and installed measured day work system and inventory
  control system and guidelines.

For a Major Office Equipment Manufacturer:
..Personally changed incentive standards to one for one system on
  various grinding operations.
..Reduced operating cost and made substantial savings by auditing
  incentive standards on machining operations.

For an Aerospace Manufacturer:
..Supervised the investigation of method difficulties in production areas, and the preparation of solution; recommendations
  involved cost adjustments of manpower, equipment and materials.
..Developed and maintained long range Division facility planning.

As an Engineering Consultant:
..Worked on task force on standard data development for all machining operations at a giant printing press manufacturer; recommendations to management involved major layout revisions,
  system changes, cost reduction methods and major operations
  changes.

For a Large Industrial Manufacturer:
..Assisted the Chief I.E. in the development and maintenance of
  the annual capital equipment expenditure budget.
..Supervised cost evaluation of new assembly line to manufacture
  saw motors and components.

AREAS OF
KNOWLEDGE AND
EXPERIENCE

Industrial Engineering	Plant Layout
	Material Handling
Work Measurement	Packaging
Time Standards, M.T.M.	Facilities Planning
Standard Data, Methods	Manpower Control
Cost Reduction	New Equipment Justification
Estimates	
	Staff Supervision
Wage Incentives	Hiring
Project Engineering	Training
Cost and Economic Analysis	

| PERSONAL | Birthdate: 4-27-45 | Married, Family |
| | 6'   200 Lbs. | Excellent health |

EDUCATION   Ohio State University, Columbus, Ohio (1965-1969)
  B.S. Degree - 1969
    Major: Industrial Management with Industrial Engineering
Special Training:
  Rochester Institute of Technology: Current I.E. Techniques
    - 1983
  Xerox Corporation: M.T.M. - 1979
  Rockwell International: Operations Research - 1978

PROFESSIONAL   American Institute of Industrial Engineers: Senior Member
MEMBERSHIPS   The Society of Manufacturing Engineers: Senior Member

EXPERIENCE
Sept., 1984   U.S. CHEMICAL AND PLASTICS, INC.
to Present

Position: Manager of Industrial Engineering

Responsibilities:
-- Appraise and recommend organization structures and functional
   assignments.
-- Set up and direct performance measurement systems.
-- Initiate, develop and maintain present and new systems and
   procedures for incentives, work analysis, estimates, costs
   and methods.
-- Directly supervise the various activities of the time study,
   project and process Industrial Engineers and technicians.

1979-1984   XEROX CORPORATION

Position: Industrial Engineer

Responsibilities:
-- Formulate methods and techniques for developing integrated
   work measurement/methods improvement systems.
-- Install and maintain systems to utilize manpower more effectively and provide for the installation of improved and standardized methods.
-- Apply industrial engineering techniques of operational analysis, methods, improvement and work measurement.
-- Analyze operating situations and recommend solutions or improvements in attaining best use of manpower resources.

1977-1979   ROCKWELL INTERNATIONAL AEROSPACE DIV.

Position: Project Industrial Engineer

Responsibilities:
-- Implement projects to develop and install integrated systems
   which measure labor output and improve manpower utilization;
   establish the best method for performing operations.

-- Conduct industrial engineering studies to define basic organizations relationships and activities; develop plans of action for conducting project activities.
-- Demonstrate to supervision and employees that the approved work measurement program is a necessary, fair, and sound basis for attaining the most effective use of manpower.
-- Provide advice and counsel to supervision and functional management concerning the interpretation and use of work measurement cost and performance statements; establish labor cost and performance goals for measured groups.

1975-1977   CONTINENTAL CONSULTANTS

Position: Industrial Engineering Consultant

Responsibilities:
-- Develop standard data for machining operations at the Harris Seybold Corporation utilizing time studies and general purpose data including collection and analysis of raw data with the aid of straight line equations (method of least squares) to the completion of standard rate form.
-- Develop and apply standard data to: engine lathes; screw machines; milling machines; planers; planer mills; boring mills; grinding machines; numeri-control machines.

1972-1975   A. O. SMITH CORPORATION

Position: Senior Industrial Engineer

Responsibility:
-- Set incentive standards for the final assembly of jet pump fractional motors with time studies and M.T.M. analysis.
-- Make cost reduction studies.
-- Estimate new jobs.
-- Develop standard data through the usage of time studies and M.T.M. patterns.
-- Set up progressive assembly line for saw motors.

1969-1972   FISHER BODY DIV. OF GENERAL MOTORS

Position: Labor Standards Analyst

TRAVEL   Agreeable to any normal travel required -- up to 50%.

LOCATION   Willing to relocate.

AVAILABILITY   3-4 weeks' notice required.

EMPLOYER   Present employer is not aware of decision to consider change
CONTACT   and may not be contacted at this time.

78

GERALD W. NUMIS

1249 Sedgwick Avenue
Massillon, OH 44646
Telephone: (216) 839-6089

OBJECTIVE   <u>Senior Engineering Management</u>
                    -- Research and Development
                    -- Manufacturing

AREAS OF KNOWLEDGE AND EXPERIENCE		
Engineering Supervision		Mechanical Engineering
Organization		Electrical Engineering
Negotiation		
		Scheduling
Budgets		Analysis
Contracts		
		R & D Projections
Project Engineering		Testing, Evaluation
Research & Development		Specifications
Feasibility Studies		
Sales Projections		Facilities Planning
Machinery Design		Supervisory Training
Product Machinery Design		Computer Usage

EXPERIENCE
April, 1981
to Present

TORMAY, INC., Massillon, OH
Manufacturers of food processing machinery.
Sales volume $9 million.

<u>Position</u>: Director of Engineering

<u>Responsibilities</u>:
    -- Set up and organize, for a brand new Company, the Engineer-
       ing, Purchasing and Inventory Departments.
    -- Design and prepare specifications for Company products.
    -- Coordinate engineering functions with other Departments.
    -- Buy or build engineering equipment.
    -- Handle mechanical and electrical engineering, cost reduc-
       tion, plant safety and OSHA.

<u>Achievements</u>:
    -- Successfully initiated and completed engineering for produc-
       tion; organized a productive operation with a capable staff.
    -- Maintained profitable production cost levels for 5 years
       through a cost reduction plan.
    -- Supervised the design of 3 new products; all were marketed
       and now produce 40% of Company total sales.

1979-1981   CONTINENTAL CAN CO. TECHNICAL CENTER, Chicago.
             Manufacturer of production machinery.

             Position: Designer II

             Responsibilities:
              -- For each design project; handle research, design analysis,
                 design, assembly and testing, critical analysis and produc-
                 tion drawings.

             Achievements:
              -- Designed a more efficient powder dispenser.
              -- Researched powder transfer characteristics and the field
                 charge of powder to enhance powder flow through tubes,
                 fluidized beds and storage bins.
              -- Redesigned the body making section of a metal can making
                 machine to increase reliability and speed.

             Reason for Change: Accepted opportunity for management responsi-
             bilities with increased earnings.

1970-1979   NATIONAL CYLINDER GAS CO., DIVISION OF CHEMTRON CORP., Elk Grove
             Village, Illinois. Makers of production machinery for the steel
             industry.

(1976-1979) Position: Research Mechanical Design Engineer

             Responsibilities:
              -- Full responsibility for assigned projects, including re-
                 search, analysis and design.

             Achievements:
              -- Worked with contract electronic engineers to design and de-
                 velop a tape controlled flame-cutting machine including a
                 mini-computer, which eliminated the need for tape preparation
                 by a service company.
              -- Designed an auto-piecing unit which controlled flame tempera-
                 ture and oxygen pressure for piercing holes in thick plate.

(1973-1976) Position: Machine Designer

             Responsibilities:
              -- Basically similar to 1976-79 duties, plus cost estimating,
                 pricing and customer contact.

             Achievements:
              -- Personally designed a special Lance Manipulator for the steel
                 making industry.
              -- Worked with electronics firm to design a line following de-
                 vice for use on the flame-cutting machine.

80

(1970-1973)	Position: Senior Draftsman

Responsibilities:
-- Prepare drawings, bills of material and the machinery design.
-- Build prototype, test and make production drawings.

Achievements:
-- Designed a flame cutting machine and flame cutting torch.
-- Designed a multiple torch for chamfering on corners for use on flame cutting unit.
-- With an electronic firm, developed a wheel driven line tracer.

1965-1970	ALLIS CHALMERS MFG. CO., Research and Development, Harvey, Illinois. Manufacturer of diesel engines.

Position: Supervisor, R & D Laboratory; Draftsman

Responsibilities and Achievements:
-- Test engines; manufacture and install experimental parts.
-- Supervise 15 employees.
-- Set up an R & D laboratory with 2 dynomometers; established an engine rebuilding department; set up a machine shop.
-- Tested and analyzed results for a new diesel engine design.

1962-1965	TURK MANUFACTURING CO. - Project Engineer ARMOUR LABORATORIES - Junior Plant Layout Engineer A. O. SMITH CORP. - Junior Tool Designer

EDUCATION	University of Illinois, Champaign, Illinois - 2 years
	Illinois Institute of Technology, Chicago, Illinois - Evening Division
	    Total of 140 credit hours
	Special Training: Northwestern University
	    Supervisory Development Program

TRAVEL	Agreeable to any moderate travel required by the position.
LOCATE	Prefer to remain in the Ohio area.
AVAILABILITY	3-4 weeks' notice required.
EMPLOYER CONTACT	Present employer is not aware of a decision to consider change and may not be contacted at this time.
REFERENCES	References available on request.

HARVEY L. CORBETT

207 White Haven Drive
Denver, CO 80114
Telephone: (303) 236-4589

OBJECTIVE

Director of Finance

HIGHLIGHTS OF
FINANCIAL/
MANAGEMENT
CAREER

As Associate Director - Holy Trinity Hospital, Denver

Financial Administration:

..Prepared $6.6 million operating and cash flow budget; $200,000 capital expenditures budget.
..Established an accounting system and rate structure to fund depreciation; used funded depreciation plus earned interest over a 4-year period to pay off a loan of $645,000.
..Set up Hospital Authority No. 1, Buffalo County, Colorado to issue tax exempt revenue bonds to fund a building project.
..Directed preparation of a Hill Burton resume and a 3% loan subsidy and grant, which was approved.
..First in Colorado to request Medicare reimbursement through the P.I.P. method; increased cash flow by $100,000.
..Prepared budget and participated in application for HMO grant funded by Westinghouse, Prudential and Blue Cross Blue Shield.
..Negotiated financing to have only $9 per patient day debt service on $5.5 million project.

Building Project: $5.5 million:

..Worked with Hospital's lay Board of Directors in design and development of the building project.
..Participated in a financing feasibility study by A. T. Kearney.
..Participated with A. G. Becker in issuing $5.5 million tax exempt revenue hospital authority bonds at 6-3/8% melted yield.
..Personally negotiated financing with tax exempt revenue bonds; resulted in a $2 million savings over the 30-year term.
..Worked with Standard and Poor; obtained A rating on bonds.
..Handled acceptance of building completion in phases; obtained Medicare reimbursement, depreciation and interest for one year during construction; resulted in $278,000 capitalization during construction.
..Purchased land and set up subdivision for building; projected savings of $40,000 by timely purchase.

Administrative/Operations:

..Developed departments and hired Directors: Personnel, Social
  Service, Credit and Collection, Purchasing.
..Hired first Directors for departments: Nursing Service, EKG,
  Physical Therapy, Respiratory Therapy, Central Stores.
..Developed a computerized system which handles a full scale ac-
  counting, medical census and utilization review certifications.
..With legal counsel, established broad range of medical and
  nursing services.
..Coordinated development of preventive maintenance program.
..Held department head turnover rate below both national and area
  averages.
..Implemented employee fringe benefit program.

Professional Activities:

..First chairman of Finance Committee for Sisters of Saint Fran-
  cis of Goldmine Springs; established pooled investments for the
  Order.
..Secretary of 3 member Central District Evaluation Board of
  Colorado Reimbursement Plan.
..Chairman (twice) District IV Colorado Hospital Association.
..Chairman (twice) Central District H.F.M.A.
..Vice President, Mountain Chapter H.F.M.A.
..Advisor, Blue Cross Blue Shield shared computer services.

AREAS OF KNOWLEDGE AND EXPERIENCE		
	Administration	Securities Portfolios
	Organization	Banking
	Financing:	Leasing
	Inventory, Accounts	Short Term Loans
	Receivables, Forms	Long Term Bonds
	Accounting	Consumer Credit
	Investments	Insurance Loans
	Financial Analysis	Federal Loans
	Financial Projections	Construction Contracts
	Budgets, Cash Flow	
		Staff Supervision
	Insurance	Personnel Policies
	Medicare Reimbursement	
	Prospective Rate Setting	Community Relations

PROFESSIONAL
MEMBERSHIPS

National Accounting Association
Colorado Banking Association
Hospital Financial Management Association
    Rocky Mountain Chapter
Colorado Hospital Association
Colorado Reimbursement Plan Evaluation Board

EDUCATION	University of Denver - 4 years
	Bachelor of Science in Business Administration - 1971
	University of Colorado - Graduate study, 1 year

Special Training:
  University of Colorado School of Business - Seminars (1985,
    1984, 1983, 1982, 1981): "Current Issues in Health Care and
    Reimbursement"

| EXPERIENCE 1977 to Present | HOLY TRINITY HOSPITAL, Denver, Colorado |
| | 127 bed acute general hospital. |

Position: Associate Director: Financial, Administrative

Responsibilities:
-- Carry out policies of Board of Directors, and insure that
   Board's objectives are met.
-- Provide leadership to insure viability; recommend policies,
   implement; supervise 23 department heads.
-- Direct and manage day-to-day operations of the hospital.
-- Vice Chairman, Finance Committee and Building Committee.
-- Treasurer, Board of Directors, from inception of the Board
   to present; participated in development of first lay Board
   of the hospital.
-- Ex-officio member, Capital Expenditure Committee of the
   Medical staff.

Prior Experience

Banking Internal Auditor: Colorado Industrial Bank, Denver
  Colorado 1975-1977
Royalty and Tax Accountant: Texaco Oil Company, Denver Regional
  Office 1973-1975
Controller: Securities Credit Corporation, Denver Office 1971-
  1973.

| PERSONAL | Birthdate: 3-12-41 | Married, Two children |
| | 5'10"   175 Lbs. | Excellent Health |

AVAILABILITY   45-60 days' notice required.

LOCATION   Willing to relocate

EMPLOYER
CONTACT   Present employer may be contacted at any time.

REFERENCES   Available upon request.

HENRY G. McKENZIE

18 West Kostbury Drive
Winston Salem, NC 28217
Telephone (281) 394-2891

OBJECTIVE

<u>Chief Executive or Chief Operating Officer</u>
-- Hard Goods Manufacturing

AREAS OF
KNOWLEDGE

General Management
Policy Determination
Operations Management

Marketing
Sales Management, Promotion
Product Development
Pricing and Margins

Customer and Public Relations
Union Negotiation

Cash Flow
Budgets and Forecasts

Manufacturing - Production
Tool and Industrial Engineering

Quality Control
Technical Applications
Cost Control

Tools and Dies
Metal Stampings, Plastics

Material Handling Equipment
Automotive Safety Equipment

Federal Highway Safety

EDUCATION

School of Trade and Commerce, Cologne, Germany
4 Year Graduate: Tool and Die Maker
                 Tool and Die Designer
Michigan State University, East Lansing, Michigan - 2 years

EXPERIENCE
1976 to
Present

MAJOR PRODUCER OF AUTOMOTIVE AND RECREATIONAL VEHICLE SAFETY
EQUIPMENT. Manufacturing Division of diversified $100 million
industrial corporation.

<u>Position</u>: Executive Vice President and General Manager

<u>Responsibilities</u>: Chief Executive Officer of the Division. Sales
of over $25 million, 450 employees. Responsible for the profit
performance of the Division, Growth Planning and all Operations,
including Manufacturing and Sales.

Achievements:
-- Guided Division from marginal earnings in 1976 and 1977 to 36% sales increases and $800,000 earnings on operations in 1978.
-- Established competitive bidding principle in Purchasing, saving $265,000 in 2 years.
-- $225,000 capital investment in equipment netted $196,000 savings in direct labor, 1977-78.
-- Reduced total inventory by 30% through EDP usage.
-- Designed and implemented new manufacturing standards and cost controls.
-- Substantially reduced turnover and absenteeism by negotiating new 3-year labor contract.
-- Initiated Sales Forecasting and Operating Budgets.
-- Established a new market which in 18 months provided $2 million in Sales and $180,000 in Earnings.
-- Installed Plant Safety Program: saved $10,000 annually on Workmen's Compensation.

1973-1976   LANSING DIVISION, A. J. INDUSTRIES, Lansing, Michigan. Manufacturer of material handling equipment, automotive and railroad. Annual sales $5.5 million, 220 employees.

(1975-1976)   Position: General Manager

Responsibilities: Profit Accountability, Growth Planning, Finance, Budgets, Sales, Marketing, Promotion, Product and Industrial Engineering, Purchasing, Materials Control, Manufacturing, Personnel, Labor Relations, Safety.

Achievements:
-- Reversed a $900,000 loss in 1973 to a marginal profit in 1974-75. Reduced sales to $3.5 million by eliminating unprofitable items.
-- Saved $300,000 by rearranging and trimming product line.
-- Established "hard-core" budgets and manufacturing labor performance standards.
-- Established a Purchasing Department: $120,000 savings.
-- Reduced raw material inventory by 21%.

(1973-1975)   Position: Chief Engineer

Responsibilities: Tooling and Manufacturing methods, Capital Requisitions, Proprietary Product Design, R & D, Customer Consultation, Quality Control, Manufacturing Cost Control, Industrial Engineering, Manufacturing Standards, Industrial Safety.

Achievements:
-- Created annual labor savings of $75,000 through conversion to semi-automatic welding production line, continuous wire-feed weld system, tooling and method process.
-- Changed single operation tools to punch press: saved $38,000 in labor and $18,000 in scrap reduction, per year.
-- Saved $26,000 in labor and reduced Inventory 12% by proper stocking and routing of raw and in-process materials.

1972-1973   LANSING STAMPING COMPANY, Lansing, Michigan. Manufacturer of automotive stampings. Annual sales $3 million.

Position: Manager, Master Mechanic Division

Responsibilities: Design, buy or build, and test all Production Tooling; supervise Tool and Die Shop. Maintain plant machinery and equipment. Responsible for product Quality Control.

Achievements:
-- Converted to full automatic transfer system from single operations, resulting in 120% production increase and first year savings of $56,000.
-- Saved $16,000 first year with electronic sensitizor inspection.

1968-1972   CONWAY COMPANY, Lansing, Michigan. Tool and Die Manufacturer.

Partner-Manager, handling Tool and Machine Design, Sales, Marketing and Promotion. Sold interest at a capital gain.

1961-1968   OLOFFSON CORPORATION, Lansing, Michigan. Builders of Tools, Dies and Machinery. Sales of $8 million.

Positions: Tool and Die Maker, Tool and Die Designer, and General Foreman.

AVAILABILITY   Subject to 4-week notice.

EMPLOYER
CONTACT   Present employer is not aware of decision to change and may not be contacted at this time.

REFERENCES   Excellent business and personal references are available upon request.

CLIFFORD V. MARSTON

2130 North Lincoln Park
Pittsburgh, PA 24022
Telephone: (281) 525-1077

OBJECTIVE   General Management/Marketing/Manufacturing

HIGHLIGHTS OF   As General Manager:
CAREER   * In first 6 months, increased unit volume 20%, dollar volume
BACKGROUND   48% and tripled pre-tax net profit, compared to same period
                         of previous year.
                       * In 6 months, Division earned more net profit before tax than
                         in either of the 2 prior full years.

                     As Director of Marketing:
                       * Reversed a trend of declining sales and profits.
                       * Increased dollar sales 25% and pre-tax profit from 3.4% to
                         6.39%, from 4th Quarter 1982 to 4th Quarter 1983.
                       * 1st Quarter 1984 performance vs. 1st Quarter 1983 was a 67%
                         sales increase with quadrupled profit before taxes; increased
                         margin on sales from 3.4% to 9.2%.

                     As Assistant to the President:
                       * Introduced a Market Mission planning concept.
                       * Implemented an integrated Comprehensive Business Planning
                         System for 1 year and 5 year revolving plans.

                     As Director of Project Offices:
                       * Successfully directed a program management operation involv-
                         ing Division contracts of $120 million annual sales.
                       * With gross profit responsibility, built an organization of 55
                         employees, primarily professional engineers.
                       * Reduced system contracts in "shipped but not billed" status
                         from an average of $7 million to a $1-2 million range.
                       * Reduced time span for review and final acceptance of con-
                         tracts from 3-4 weeks to 6-8 days.

                     As Director of Management Services:
                       * Developed and implemented a framework of management controls
                         for budgets, forecasts and business planning, delegation of
                         authority, performance reporting for technical, scheduling
                         and financial areas, project initiation, problem anticipa-
                         tion and exception reporting.

                     As Director of Manufacturing and Materials:
                       * Organized the total manufacturing operation, involving $2.8
                         million in annual costs.
                       * Introduced data processing for inventory control and project
                         monitoring.
                       * Placed over 100 product models in production while remaining
                         well under shop cost budget.

AREAS OF KNOWLEDGE AND EXPERIENCE	General Management	Marketing/Sales Management
	Full Profit Responsibility	Product Line Development
	Policy Determination	Pricing and Margins
	Operating Procedures	Research and Development
	Business, Profit Planning	Engineering
	Budgets, Forecasts	Computer Usage
	Project Management	Manufacturing, Production
	Problem Solving	Inventory
	Cost Control	Purchasing
	MIS Applications	

EDUCATION

Case Institute of Technology, Cleveland, Ohio
   M.S. Degree in Electrical Engineering - 1964
University of Wisconsin, Madison, Wisconsin
   B.S. Degree in Electrical Engineering - 1958
Special Training: Marquette University, Lawrence College,
   San Diego State College, American Management Association.

EXPERIENCE

Oct., 1982 to Present

DONWELL INDUSTRIES, Peotone, PA
Multiplant manufacturer of plastic and steel shipping containers.

(Dec., 1983 to Present)

Position: General Manager, Container Division
Responsibilities:
-- Full profit responsibility for the Division. Direct Sales and Marketing. Quality Assurance and Manufacturing operations (600 employees, 360,000 sq. ft.). Four main product lines (steel pails, steel drums, injection molded plastic pails, blow molded closed head plastic containers). Eight plants in 4 locations. $57 million sales.

(Oct., 1982- Dec., 1983)

Position: Director of Marketing
Responsibilities:
-- Reorganized and rebuilt the Department. Recruited Regional and District Sales Managers. Established policies and procedures and a sense of discipline and goals. Improved delivery performance.

1978-1982

DAILEY RETER COMPANY, Wickliffe, Ohio
Subsidiary of Babcox-Wilcox, Manufacturer of Instrumentation and controls for steam electric power generation.

(1979-1982)

Position: Vice President of Planning and Development
Responsibilities:
-- Defined crucial problems and opportunities facing the Company. Directed planning activities within 3 profit centers and 2 separate ventures. Made financial analysis of all proposed plans. Chairman of Product Planning Committee. Responsible for R & D coordination and capital equipment investment program. Bottom line responsibility for Automation Center separate venture. Contract Administrator for Government sponsored R & D contracts.

(1978-1979)   Position: Manager, Digital System Department
Responsibilities:
-- Organized the efforts of the Company in completion and installation of a new proprietary digital control computer
system that was far behind schedule for 12 systems already
sold.

(1978)   Position: Assistant to the President
Responsibilities:
-- Implemented a task force to identify problems in the business; formulated an action plan. Helped reorganize the Company from a functional concept to profit centers.

1969-1978   CONTROL DATA CORPORATION

(1977-1978)   Position: Director of Project Offices
Development and Standard System Division
Responsibilities:
-- Gross profit responsibility for program management operation
of Company's Standard Computer System contracts. Formulated
and implemented approved policy and price structure on OEM
sales of Company's 1700 computer products. Held inventory
levels below budget.

Prior Positions: Development and Standard System Division:
Director of Management Services

Control Systems Division:
Director of Manufacturing and Material
Manager, Technical Services
Chief Application Engineer
Chief Systems Analyst
Systems Analyst

1964-1969   CREOLE PETROLEUM CORPORATION, Caracas, Venezuela

Position: Automation Engineer
Responsibilities:
-- As Development Engineer in systems engineering, coordinated
automation projects and studies in oil production operation,
instrumentation and control techniques and investigation of
electrical field developments.

ELIZABETH KINKAID

3401 South Swan Island
Eugene, OR 91412
Telephone: (206) 947-2611

OBJECTIVE

Hospitality Management
-- Assistant Motel Manager
-- Food and Beverage/Convention Management

HIGHLIGHTS OF
MOTEL
MANAGEMENT
EXPERIENCE

As Motel Manager of Two Motels $900,000 annual Volume

.. Attracted a better clientele by upgrading all areas of motel operations.
.. Achieved harmony among a harder working staff.
.. Decreased payroll on weekends by new working schedule; saved salary of 2 clerks.
.. Reduced front desk cash shortages by improving caliber of personnel.
.. Lowered supplies costs by better control over inventory and shopping for lower prices.
.. Increased collections of rent and telephone charges.
.. Eliminated use of non-paid rooms through improved security and by establishing excellent relations with local police.

AREAS OF
KNOWLEDGE

Motel Management

General Management
Profit Responsibility
Room Rentals

Staff Supervision
Hiring
Training
Work Planning, Scheduling

Front Desk Operations
Reservations
Credit Approval
Cashiering
Accounts Receivable

Personnel

Cost Control
Purchasing
Inventory Control

Maintenance Direction
Decorating
Administrative Housekeeping
Improvements

Union Relations

Community Relations
Sales Promotion

Personal Hospitality
Guest Relations

MANAGEMENT
CHARACTERISTICS

Successful motel operations: sales, profit.
Profit oriented; cost conscious.
Personal flair for hospitality.
Labor efficiencies a must.
Full knowledge of value of Sales Promotion.

PERSONAL   Birthdate: 12-29-60   Single
                  5'4-1/2"   120 Lbs.   Excellent health

EDUCATION   Thornton Community College, South Holland, Oregon - 1 year
                      Currently attending. Major: Business Administration
                  Special Training: Interior Decorating

EXPERIENCE
Sept., 1978   DUNES MOTEL, 3401 South Swan Island, Eugene 91412
to Present   THUNDERBIRD MOTEL, 4501 South Short Drive, Eugene 91412
                  Dunes' annual sales volume over $375,000; Thunderbird volume
                  over $525,000 total of 50 employees.

(Jan., 1984   Position: Motel Manager - 2 Motels
to Present
                  Responsibilities:
                  -- Manage the two motels, with full profit responsibilities;
                     supervise a total staff of 50 employees.
                  -- Direct all operations: front desk, personnel, housekeeping,
                     maintenance, security.
                  -- Handle payroll, accounts receivable, partial accounts payable.
                  -- Build good relations with clientele and employees.

(Jan., 1982-   Position: Assistant Motel Manager: Dunes Motel
Jan., 1984)
                  Responsibilities:
                  -- Substantially manage the motel, due to the absence of the
                     Manager (who also managed another motel).
                  -- Direct all front desk operations: reservations, room assign-
                     ments, hiring, training, switchboard and some purchasing.
                  -- Manage and supervise the maintenance and housekeeping acti-
                     vities.

                  Achievements:
                  -- Increased total motel sales volume on an annual basis, in
                     spite of serious downturn in the U.S. economy.
                  -- Introduced an effective system which controlled and reduced
                     the loss of keys.

(March, 1980   Position: Head Housekeeper
Jan., 1982)

(Sept., 1978   Position: Desk Clerk/Switchboard Operator
March 1980)

EMPLOYER   Present employer may be contacted at any time.
CONTACT

HUGH R. BURTON, M.D.

1409 South Steward Avenue
Houston, TX 52701
Telephone: (412) 728-4378

OBJECTIVE   Corporate Consultant: Industrial Medicine

AREAS OF   Human Relations   Safety
KNOWLEDGE   General Medicine and Surgery   Motivational Techniques
AND   Industrial Medicine   Costs
EXPERIENCE   Compensation Medicine   Budgetary Control

                     Hospital Administration   Record Retrieval
                     Facility Planning   Labor Relations
                     Medical Records   O.S.H.A. Regulations
                     Industrial Hygiene

EDUCATION   University of Pittsburgh School of Medicine
                         M.D. Degree
                     University of Pittsburgh
                         B.S. Degree   Major: Pre-Medical
                     Special Training:
                         University of Pennsylvania Evening Extension Division:
                             Accounting - 2 yrs.; Contract Law - 1 yr.;
                             Economics - 2 yrs.

PROFESSIONAL   Western States Society of Industrial Medicine and Surgery
MEMBERSHIPS   Industrial Medical Association

EXPERIENCE
Oct., 1981   FRANKLIN PARK INDUSTRIAL CLINIC, Houston, Texas
Nov., 1986   Clinic provides industrial patient care for 500 companies.
                     Position: Industrial Physician

                     Responsibilities: Provide good medical care to industrial
                     patients of client companies. In the absence of the Clinic
                     Director, handle administrative and business problems.

July, 1971   U.S. STEEL CORPORATION - Joliet Works
Oct., 1981   Steel Fabricating plant. 1600 employees.

                     Position: Plant Medical Director

                     Responsibilities: Provide necessary emergency, surgical,
                     medical and rehabilitative care of U.S. Steel employees
                     injured or ill on the job.

                     Achievements:
                     -- Set objectives for reducing cost of Employee Medical
                        Benefits Program for two years, the first year by 25%
                        and the second year by 10%; met both objectives.

-- Changed the medical records from an individual sheet of paper for each incident with multiple copies, to a single, chronological, continuous record of medical incidents for each individual with a single carbon copy of separate incidents.
-- Developed a Keysort system for local use for keeping the department informed of times for periodic exams, immunizations and other pertinent medical data.
-- Presented a Medical Self-Help program for national or local disasters to Management, employees and the community.
-- Installed an effective filing system; culled the medical record files; sent older pertinent material to a central corporate storage area for 50-year storage.

Dec., 1969
April, 1971

STONEBROD STEEL COMPANY, Milligahagen, Pennsylvania
Fully integrated steel company. 3,000 employees.

Position: Corporate Medical Director

Responsibilities and Achievements:
-- Developed a corporate medical policy to provide improved medical/surgical/rehabilatitive care to employees injured or ill on the job; covered main steel mill, private railroad company and two mines.
-- Created a Management Job Clarification outline for a Medical Director with performance standards for each responsiblity.
-- Completely revised the medical record system including reports sent to operating, safety, accounting and compensation departments.
-- Drew up plans and costs for a modern medical dispensary to provide more efficient medical services.

1967
1969

A. F. OF L. MEDICAL CENTER OF PHILADELPHIA
Medical clinic for Union members; 60,000 eligible members.

Position: Medical Director

Responsibilities and Achievements:
-- Select, consult, advise, direct and control a medical staff of 60 physicians representing 26 medical specialties and subspecialties.
-- Administer and control the nursing, laboratory, physical therapy and medical record staffs.
-- Completely revised the medical record department so that storage, retrieval and delivery of 37,000 patient medical records were immediately available as required.

| 1964 | MIDDLETON MEDICAL COLLEGE AND HOSPITAL OF PHILADELPHIA |
| 1966 | 500 bed hospital |

Position: Director of Professional Services and Associate Medical Director

Responsibilities and Achievements:
-- Manage and control the administrative services of the hospital; admissions office, medical records, food service, out-patient department, nursing staff.
-- Manage the Intern and Resident staffs; procurement, training, control, educational programs.
-- Maintain liaison with Active Staff, Courtesy Staff and the College Administration.
-- Obtained a 100% quota of Interns in a difficult period.
-- Improved admitting procedure of patients; rearranged the facilities in the Out-Patient Department; administered a methods improvement program for the service staff personnel.
-- Improved the meal delivery system in the 18-story hospital to provide hot meals.

| 1961 | THE READING HOSPITAL, Reading, PA 500 bed hospital. |
| 1964 | |

Position: Medical Director

Responsibilities and Achievements:
-- Direct the activities of the medical staff; control, evaluate, enforce regulations and discipline.
-- Correlate staff training activities to conform to state and national standards; administer the employee health clinic and health program for the School of Nursing.
-- Maintain liaison between the medical staff and the Hospital administration staff.
-- Edited and coordinated material for a 144-page Resident Staff manual for medical management in all the specialties.

| 1955 | Private Medical Practice, Vincennes, Indiana. |
| 1960 | |

JANET B. LUPTON

4312 Merrivale Road
Los Angeles, CA 90126
Telephone: (210) 421-6679

OBJECTIVE
Underwriting Management or Supervision
-- Casualty Insurance or Reinsurance

AREAS OF
KNOWLEDGE
AND
EXPERIENCE

Workmen's Compensation
General Liability
Automobile, Including Truckmen
Umbrella Liability
Fidelity
Crime Coverages
Directors and Officers
   Liability
Inland Marine
Fire and Allied Lines
Commercial Package

Large Risk Rating Techniques
Loss Rating
Retrospective Rating
Aggregate and Specific Excess
Cash Flow Plans

Staff Supervision
Manpower Development
Salary Administration

PERSONAL
Birthdate: 12-12-53   Single
5'6"   130 Lbs.   Excellent health

EDUCATION
Loyola University, Chicago, Illinois - 4 years
   B. A. Degree
      Major: Speech   Minor: Philosophy

PROFESSIONAL
MEMBERSHIP

American Society for Training and Development

EXPERIENCE
March, 1984
May, 1986

HARBOR INSURANCE COMPANY/UNION AMERICA INSURANCE GROUP,
Los Angeles, CA
Property and casualty insurance; emphasis on industrial,
commercial and contracting risks. $95 million direct pre-
mium written.

Position: Underwriter

Responsibilities:
-- Basically responsible for the selection and pricing of
   casualty business.
-- Handle all standard policyholder services functions.

Achievements:
-- Personally assumed policyholder services functions previously handled by President of related wholesale
   brokerage firm; part of Company's growth effort toward
   Directors and Officers Liability Insurance.

96

-- Full exposure to the Agency business.
-- Participated in team effort in the underwriting and production of large block of Commercial Package business, in keeping with Company's objective to produce a higher percentage of Property business.

Feb., 1982
March, 1984

ALLSTATE INSURANCE COMPANY, Northbrook, Illinois
Large insurance company; all lines.

Position: Underwriting Supervisor: Special Accounts/Large Risks

Responsibilities:
-- Direct the selection and pricing of new and renewal Casualty and Property business.
-- Supervise a staff of 2 Senior Underwriters, 2 Underwriters, 2 Technical Assistants and a clerk.
-- Handle manpower development and training, and salary administration.

Achievements:
-- Promoted from Senior Underwriter to Underwriting Division Supervisor in 4 months.
-- One of first 3 people other than Home Office staff to be given responsibility for placing facultative reinsurance.
-- Selected to participate in management review of troubled Florida Regional operations.
-- Contributed extensively to setting up Allstate's first General Agency agreement in commercial lines.
-- Cleared up substantial policy production backlog in Property lines through a manpower reorganization.

March, 1978
Feb., 1982

LIBERTY MUTUAL INSURANCE COMPANY, Chicago, Illinois
Property and casualty insurance.

(Aug., 1980
Feb., 1982)

Position: Supervising Underwriter

Responsibilities:
-- Direct and manage a Casualty and Property Underwriting Unit; new and renewal business in a 4-state territory.
-- Coordinate basic training program; handle numerous special assignments.
-- Supervise 3 Underwriters, 2 Technical Assistants and a clerk.

Achievements:
-- Territory under personal supervision exceeded 15% growth objective both years; consistently produced an underwriting profit.
-- Twice called upon to handle two supervisory territories in emergency shortages of Supervisors.
-- Promoted to Supervising Underwriter in about half the normal time required.

(Mar., 1978
Aug., 1980)

Position: Underwriter

Responsibilities:
-- Select and price new and renewal business in one state; later expanded to three.
-- Begin the coordination of a basic training program.

Achievements:
-- Ranked first among 5 trainees in 10-week Basic Training Program.
-- Handled the Missouri/Southern Illinois Territory alone, although normally assigned to 2 people.
-- Youngest person ever assigned as Training Coordinator.

LOCATE   Willing to relocate.

AVAILABILITY   Immediate.

EMPLOYER   Past employers may be contacted at any time.
CONTACT

REFERENCES   References available upon request.

JOHN J. KINSMAN

6448 Parkside Avenue
New York, NY 02166
Telephone: (201) 611-4281

OBJECTIVE   <u>Regional Director</u> or <u>Vice President, Group Sales</u>
                  -- Insurance Industry

AREAS OF   Group Life Insurance   Sales
KNOWLEDGE   Individual Life Insurance   Sales Management
                                            Sales Training

              Accident and Health Insurance
              Medical Care Insurance   Administration

EDUCATION   DePaul University, Chicago, Illinois - B.S. Degree
                  Major: Business Administration
                  Minor: Marketing

EXPERIENCE
1966 to   LEADING INSURANCE COMPANY, one of the very largest in the
Present   United States, offering complete coverage with all forms
               of life, health, hospital, and medical care insurance.

(1977 to   <u>Position</u>: Group Account Executive (Regional Office) after pro-
Present)   motion from Group Sales Supervisor. Report to Vice President.

               <u>Responsibilities</u>:
               -- To personally manage and serve the extremely large group
                  accounts; annual premiums range from $250,000 to many
                  millions.
               -- To maintain and build Company relations with Brokers and
                  Insurance Consultants.
               -- To represent the Company at the highest levels.

               <u>Achievements</u>:
               -- Successfully handled complicated claim negotiations, to the
                  satisfaction of major policy holders and the Company.
               -- Assisted in the underwriting and administrative areas, in-
                  volving the most important clients.
               -- In 1977, qualified as 4th leading Account Executive, al-
                  though in the position only a few months.

(1968-1977)   Position: Group Sales Supervisor (Minneapolis, Milwaukee Offices) after promotion from Sales Supervisor/Sales Trainee.

Responsibilities:
-- Initially, to develop Group Life Sales to new accounts, substantially opening the northern Wisconsin and Upper Michigan areas.
-- Since promotion to Milwaukee (1972), responsible for maintenance of large and vital Group accounts.
-- To train and assist Company agents in building Group Sales through prospect development.

Achievements:
-- In 1974, was 18th leading Company Sales Representative in the United States.
-- Sold over $221 million of new life insurance in 1975, climbing to No. 2 in the country.
-- Ranked first in the United States in 1976; $102 million of life insurance and $863 thousand of disability premium produced.
-- Built a reputation for achievement in personal sales along with an excellent conservation record and underwriting performance.

(1967-1968)   Position: Service Supervisor/Sales Trainee (Chicago Office), after promotion from Insurance Agent.

(1966-1967)   Position: Insurance Agent (Joliet, Illinois Office)

TRAVEL   Agreeable to any amount required to handle the position effectively.

LOCATE   Readily willing to relocate anywhere.

AVAILABILITY   30 days after final hiring commitment.

EMPLOYER CONTACT   Present employer is not aware of decision to change. Do not contact before hiring commitment.

REFERENCES   Business and personal references immediately available upon request.

JOEL CAMPBELL

199 County Line
Miami, FL 19921
Telephone: (206) 645-2937

OBJECTIVE	<u>Portfolio Management: Institutional</u> -- Bonds, Equities

HIGHLIGHTS OF CAREER BACKGROUND	* Proposed and originated corporate bond swaps involving yield pickups and sector moves, which resulted in maximizing portfolio return.

* Developed new accounts and maximized existing account production.

* Successfully counseled banks, insurance companies and pension funds on most attractive areas of fixed income investments.

* Actively discussed and implemented money management activities with accounts such as Swift Pension, CNA Bond Fund, Alliance Capital Corporation, Boatman's National Bank and St. Louis Union Trust.

* Participated in the National Bond Sales Conference.

* In first year at Drexel Firestone, developed corporate and convertible bond and preferred stock production from $200,000 to $800,000 annually.

* Was top 5% producer nationally at F. I. DuPont 1976-1979; built individual institutional sales gross profit from zero to $400,000 per year.

* During 3 years with R. S. Dickson & Company, New York City, made corporate and municipal bond sales to all major accounts to which assigned in the New York Metropolitan area.

AREAS OF KNOWLEDGE AND EXPERIENCE	Portfolio Management Bond Research	Corporate Bonds Municipal Bonds Preferred Stocks Convertible Securities
	New Business Development Client Relations	
		Corporate Bond Swapping Bond Sector Analysis
	Profit Sharing and Pension Plans Bank and Insurance Investment Laws	

PROFESSIONAL MEMBERSHIP	Bond Club of Miami

EDUCATION   Knox College, Galesburg, Illinois
                    BA Degree - 1963

EXPERIENCE
SUMMARY
1984 to   G. H. WALKER, LAIRD, INC., Miami
Present
                 Position: Corporate Bond Sales

                 Responsibilities:
                 -- Work with money and portfolio managers in the sale of
                    new issues and secondary market trading of corporate
                    bonds, preferred stocks and private placements.
                 -- Primary contacts are major banks, insurance companies,
                    state retirement funds, investment counselors and
                    corporate pension plans.

1982   BLYTH EASTMAN DILLON, Miami
1984
                 Position: Corporate Bond Sales

                 Responsibilities:
                 -- Develop corporate bond sales in a 4-state territory.
                 -- Train junior bond salesman to become a proficient pro-
                    ducer.
                 -- Act as conferee at weekly national institutional bond
                    sales meeting.

1980   DREXEL FIRESTONE, Chicago
1982
                 Position: Corporate Bond Sales

                 Responsibilities:
                 -- Assist Sales Manager to develop a viable fixed income
                    capability with emphasis on corporate bond trading.
                 -- Market institutional bond research to pension and profit
                    sharing plans.
                 -- Develop new business in corporate bond area.
                 -- Member of Chicago Committee for National Reorganization of
                    Corporate Bond Trading Department.

1973   F. I. DU PONT, Chicago
1980
                 Position: Institutional Salesman

                 Responsibilities:
                 -- Develop institutional sales capability with banks, insu-
                    rance companies and pension funds.
                 -- Market the firm's institutional research effort.
                 -- Participate, upon invitation, in Sheldon Stewart profit
                    sharing trust.

102

| 1970 | R. S. DICKSON & COMPANY, New York City |
| 1973 | |

Position: Institutional Salesman

Responsibilities:
-- Learn to work with corporate bond and municipal bond accounts.
-- Develop equity sales program.

| 1968 | THE ILLINOIS COMPANY, Chicago |
| 1970 | |

Position: Common Stock Trader and Order Clerk

Responsibilities:
-- Manage listed and unlisted stock order trading desk.
-- Trade stock positions of $100,000.
-- Develop regional dealer contacts.

| 1966 | PAINE, WEBBER, JACKSON & CURTIS, Chicago |
| 1968 | |

Position: Stock Broker Trainee

Responsibilities:
-- After a 9-month training period, manage the unlisted stock trading desk in an office with 50 salesmen, with full responsibility to execute all unlisted stock trading orders.

LOCATE   Willing to relocate.

AVAILABILITY 30 days' notice required.

EMPLOYER   Present and past employers may be contacted at any time.
CONTACT

REFERENCES   References available upon request.

JOSEPH W. OWENS

211 Indian Hill Road
Wilmette, IL 60018
Telephone: (312) 262-0098

OBJECTIVE   Director of Labor Relations

HIGHLIGHTS   As Assistant Manager, Labor Relations - Chicago
OF CAREER   * Successfully processed hundreds of grievances during
                   the past year and negotiated the resolution of many.

                 * Maintained good relationships with 3 of the largest
                   local unions in the steel industry; no wildcat strikes.

                 As Superintendent Personnel Services - Iron Mountain
                 * Built excellent rapport with both Plant Grievance Commit-
                   tee and International Union, with resulting lowest griev-
                   ance rate in Company; only 6 grievances arbitrated in 8
                   years.

                 * Negotiated comprehensive local seniority agreement with
                   2000 member local production and maintenance union.

                 * Counseled operating management in all phases of labor re-
                   lations including suspension and discharge; all such
                   problems satisfactorily resolved at plant level.

                 As Superintendent Pers. Serv. (Industrial Relations), Kenosha
                 * Negotiated a local seniority agreement which received recog-
                   nition as an industrial model.

                 * Participated in many arbitration cases, with an 80-20 win-
                   loss record.

                 * Installed complex direct labor measurement incentives with
                   minimum disputes; no run-away rates.

                 * Maintained excellent arms-length relationships with local and
                   International Union; most problems resolved in early stages
                   without resort to hard contractual adversary positions.

AREAS OF   Industrial Relations   Labor Relations Policies
KNOWLEDGE   Labor Relations   Personnel Policies
AND   Labor Negotiations   Industrial Safety
EXPERIENCE
                 Union Relations   EEOC Compliance
                 Contract Administration
                 Grievance Handling   College Recruiting Programs
                 Arbitration Preparation,   Employee Suggestion Programs
                     Presentation

104

EDUCATION Cleveland Marshall Law School, Cleveland, Ohio
          LLB Degree - 1964
          Kent State University, Kent, Ohio - 4 years
          AB Degree - 1960
          Major: Political Science   Minor: History

EXPERIENCE
SUMMARY
1961 to   COLUMBIA STEEL CORPORATION
Present
(current)   Position: Assistant Manager, Labor Relations - Chicago

              Responsibilities:
              -- Handle grievances, unresolved at plant level, with
                 International Union representatives.
              -- Develop contractual position and analysis in prepara-
                 tion for processing to arbitration. (All grievances
                 from the corporation's two major Central area plants,
                 Iron Mountain and Kenosha.)
              -- Prepare grievances for arbitration and present to Com-
                 pany Board of Arbitration.

(1973-1982)   Position: Superintendent Personnel Services - Iron Mountain

              Responsibilities:
              -- Report to Plant General Superintendent.
              -- Direct the Departmental staff of 8 employees; responsible
                 for total personnel services function.
              -- Handle Labor Relations, Personnel, Safety, Training,
                 Medical, Plant Protection, Suggestions, and all related
                 functions.

(1966-1973)   Position: Superintendent Personnel Services (Industrial Rela-
                        tions) - Kenosha

              Responsibilities:
              -- Responsible for total Industrial Relations and Personnel
                 Services function; Labor Relations, Personnel, Safety,
                 Training, Medical, Plant Protection, Suggestions, and all
                 related functions.
              -- Maintain a competent, high caliber Departmental staff of
                 8 members; plant employees totaled 2,000.

(1964-1966)   Position: Assistant Labor Relations Supvr. - Worcester, Mass.

              Responsibilities:
              -- Assist the Superintendent of Industrial Relations in resolv-
                 ing a large backlog of old grievances; involved interpreta-
                 tion and application of the steelworkers' labor agreements,
                 negotiations with the local unions and advising the local
                 management. Plant employed approximately 2,000.

(1961-1964)   <u>Position</u>: Staff Assistant, Labor Relations - Cleveland

                   <u>Responsibilities</u>:
                   -- Maintain statistics for all grievances and arbitration
                      cases in American Steel and Wire Division of Columbia
                      Steel Corp.; ranged as high as 600 cases pending.
                   -- Participate in the review of all grievances and advised
                      plants on contractual position; assist in preparation
                      of arbitration cases.

SALARY   Open to discussion, depending on position and potential.

TRAVEL   Agreeable to any moderate travel required.

LOCATE   Willing to relocate

AVAILABILITY   30 days' notice required.

EMPLOYER   Present employer is not aware of decision to consider change
CONTACT   and may <u>not</u> be contacted at this time.

REFERENCES   References are available upon request.

JENNIFER BARR

5001 South Englewood
Atlanta, GA 29706
Telephone: (404) 612-0907

OBJECTIVE   Reference Librarian: University/College

AREAS OF   Reference/Research   Budgets
KNOWLEDGE   Book Selection   Statistics Reports
AND   Report Writing
EXPERIENCE   Book Reviews
                                              Public Relations
                   Library Administration
                   Staff Supervision   Public Speaking
                   Personnel Training,
                      Evaluation   Community Involvement

                   Program Development   A-V Equipment

PERSONAL   Birthdate: 9-11-52   Single
                   5'3"   Excellent health

EDUCATION   Rosary College, River Forest, Illinois
                      M.A. Degree in Library Science - 1980
                   Loyola University, Chicago, Illinois
                      B.S. Degree in Humanities - 1976
                         Major: History   Minors: Spanish, Political Science
                   Special Training:
                      Principles of Supervision

LANGUAGES   Spanish, read and speak with moderate fluency
                   French, read.

PROFESSIONAL   American Library Association
ASSOCIATIONS   Georgia Library Association

FOREIGN   Eleven European countries, Canada, Mexico.
TRAVEL

EXPERIENCE
1979 to   ATLANTA PUBLIC LIBRARY
Present

(1983 to   Position: Branch Librarian - North Lake View Branch
Present)

107

Responsibilities:
-- Full responsibility for the operations and administration
   of an Atlanta Branch Library.
-- Supervise Library personnel; 2 professional Librarians,
   1 Para-professional, 12 full time and part time clerical
   and custodial employees.
-- Handle program planning and book selection and upkeep of
   the book, record and periodical collection -- 24,000
   total volumes.
-- Responsible for personnel training, motivation and evaluation.
-- Prepare annual budget, annual and monthly reports and
   write special reports.
-- Maintain and build good community relations; public speaking before community groups about library services.
-- Direct building maintenance activities.

Achievements:
-- Under the direction of the Branch Coordinator, assisted in
   organizing and supervising the establishment of this new
   Branch Library; helped plan the layout and floor plan;
   ordered a basic book collection of over 20,000 volumes.
-- Maintained excellent relations with community groups responsible for establishing the Branch; personal talks
   given before these groups have been well received.
-- Guided the Library staff in developing effective programs
   of direct benefit to the community and the public; North
   Lake View Branch is now one of the most active storefront
   libraries in the Atlanta Library System.
-- Initiated a series of book reviews and film presentations
   for Senior Citizen groups.
-- Maintained discipline and immaculate library premises in a
   changing neighborhood environment with close proximity to
   an elementary school.
-- Built and retained high staff morale.

Reason for Change: Desire to relocate away from Atlanta.

(1979-1983)   Position: Adult Services Librarian (Librarian I) - Bezazian
                 Branch (1980-1983)
                 Librarian Trainee (1979)

Responsibilities:
-- Handled reference/research work and assisted the public
   in searches for information and books.
-- Selected and booked films for weekly programs.
-- Prepared publicity releases; planned and built reading
   room and window exhibits and displays.
-- Processed new books.
-- Acted as Librarian in charge in the absence of the Branch
   Librarian; supervised other employees.

Achievements:

-- Instituted a series of Senior Citizens book review programs in the Uptown community; received two plaques of appreciation and many letters of commendation as a result of the programs.
-- Bezazian Branch Library received $1,000 as a result of a proposal, co-sponsored with the Children's Librarian, for special equipment to aid Senior Citizen patrons.
-- Successfully passed a Civil Service examination for Librarian II (June, 1982).

Reason for Change: Promoted to Branch Librarian, North Lake View Branch.

TRAVEL	Agreeable to any normal amount required.
LOCATION	Readily willing to relocate.
AVAILABILITY	3-4 weeks' notice necessary.
EMPLOYER CONTACT	Present employer is not aware of decision to consider change and may not be contacted at this time.
REFERENCES	Available upon request.

JEROME Y. HAVEN

498 Lafferton Road
Louisville, KY 25942
Telephone: (502) 728-1978

OBJECTIVE

Manufacturers Representative: Midwest Region
-- Emphasis on Major Steel Service Centers

HIGHLIGHTS
OF SALES
CAREER

As a Manufacturers Representative:
.. Built sales from $200,000 to over $1 million in 3 years
.. Doubled sales each year for 3 years.
.. Added record number of new accounts.
.. Sold major national steel distributors: Jos. T. Ryerson, Central Steel and Wire, A. M. Castle, E. M. Jorgenson, Service Steel.
.. Ranked No. 1 among sales agents for every year.
.. Sold at highest corporate levels, including Owners, Presidents, Vice Presidents, as well as Engineers.

For Another Manufacturer:
.. Increased sales from 0 to $250,000 per year.
.. No claims against shipments; a first in the industry.
.. Sold the toughest technical job in the industry.
.. Added more new accounts than any agent in Company history.

For a Third Manufacturer:
.. Sold a completely new concept to the Steel Service Centers in the Midwest.
.. Took a revolutionary new idea and sold approximately $500,000 of material in one year.

As a Company Sales Representative:
For a Steel Tubing Manufacturer:
.. As first Company salesman, took sales from 0 to $1 million in less than 2 years.
.. Created a new attitude toward the Company on the part of the Distributors.
.. Closed numerous industrial sales through engineering-production problem solving.

For a Steel Producer:
.. Increased sales in Region by 40% per year.
.. Set Company record for new accounts first year.
.. Successfully sold major corporations: Caterpillar, International Harvester.

AREAS OF KNOWLEDGE AND EXPERIENCE	Sales Administration, Supervision Marketing Product Line Development Personal Selling of Key Accounts National Account Contact Industrial Sales OEM Accounts Specification Sales Customer Relations	Pricing Sales Budgeting Sales Forecasting Territory Layout Distributor Set-up, Contact, Control Trade Shows Engineer Liaison

PERSONAL   Birthdate: 9-10-48   Married, 2 Children
           6'   165 Lbs.   Excellent health

EDUCATION Ohio State University, Columbus, Ohio
             Major: English   Minor: International Studies

MEMBERSHIPS   Steel Service Center Institute
CERTIFICATION Welded Steel Tube Institute
              Private Pilot Single Engine Land License

EXPERIENCE
AS SALES
AGENT
1980 to   WELDED TUBES, INC., Orwell, Ohio
Present   Manufacturer of welded steel tubing. Sales volume $5 million.
(concurrent)

1981 to   VALMONT INDUSTRIES, INC., Valley, Nebraska.
Present   Manufacturer of steel tubing, irrigation systems, lighting
(concurrent) poles. Sales volume $70 million.

1985 to   CHANDLER EXPANDED METALS, Chandler, Oklahoma.
Present   Manufacturer of expanded metal.
(concurrent)

             Position: Sales Agent

             Responsibilities:
             -- Full personal responsibility for marketing and sales in
                the Chicago and/or Midwest area; 8 state basic territory.
             -- Administration, pricing, specifications, financial, col-
                lections, claim adjustment, customer service and customer
                relations.

1980   DIAL TUBE & METAL COMPANY, Dallas, Texas
1981   Sales Agency. Volume $2 million.

             Position: Sales Agent - Chicago/Midwest
                       Handle all marketing for the Midwest Region.

| 1978 | VULCAN TUBE & METAL, Chicago Heights, Illinois. |
| 1980 | Manufacturer of welded steel tubing. Volume $3 million. |

Position: Sales Representative - Midwest Region

| 1973 | REPUBLIC STEEL COMPANY, Cleveland, Ohio. |
| 1978 | |

Position: Sales Representative - Illinois

COMMISSION
CONTRACT   Agreeable to commission rates normal for the industry.

TRAVEL   Agreeable to extensive travel in Midwest areas now
                  covered.

AVAILABILITY   Immediate.

EMPLOYER   Present manufacturers are aware of decision to add one or
CONTACT   more new lines and may be contacted at any time.

REFERENCES   References are available upon request.

KENNETH C. MITCHELL

4217 New Manor Drive
Jackson, KS 41798
Telephone: (713) 273-9110

OBJECTIVE   Senior Management: Operations/Manufacturing/Engineering

HIGHLIGHTS   As Plant Manager
OF CAREER   * Successfully accomplished plant turn around from
                     $6 million loss (in last 3 years) to a profit.
                   * Developed operating procedures for efficient use of elec-
                     trical power which provided annual savings of $97,000.
                   * Increased production and reduced plant operating costs
                     through use of budgets, management by objectives and de-
                     tailed cost control; savings in thousands. Developed
                     standards of performance.
                   * Expanded production 10% over rated plant capacity.
                   * Developed, tested and installed fuel economy improve-
                     ments which will result in annual savings of up to
                     $85,000.
                   * Turned around a bad labor climate at two plants; improved
                     morale and individual productivity.

                   As Engineer - Operations Staff, Corporate Headquarters
                   * Developed corporate-wide maintenance control program to
                     permit management at plant level; results were efficient
                     use of manpower, less equipment downtime, increased pro-
                     duction, and reliable forecasting of future maintenance
                     requirements.
                   * Established electrical testing and inspection which lowered
                     downtime and improved production.

                   As Resident Engineer
                   * Directed construction and startup of 3 new cement plants:
                     $13 million project - 1.25 million barrel dry process
                     plant; $18 million project - 1.8 million barrel wet pro-
                     cess plant; $23 million project - 3.3 million barrel wet
                     process plant.
                   * Administered $8 million in cost plus contracts on one
                     project.

                   As Field Engineer
                   * Coordinated activities of contractors in 3 projects total-
                     ing $20 million.
                   * Supervised complete projects; concrete foundation, steel
                     and machinery erection, electrical and instrumentation in-
                     stallation, check out and start up operations.

113

AREAS OF KNOWLEDGE AND EXPERIENCE	Operations Administration	Construction
	Plant Management	Project Management
	Manufacturing, Production	Engineering; Mechnical, Electrical, Civil, Maintenance
	Production Standards	Machinery
	Production Control	
	Purchasing	Field Supervision
	Quality Control	Installation
	Labor Relations	Start Up
	Organizational Structure	Staff Supervision
	Operating Procedures	Hiring
	Projections	Training
	Budgeting	
	Cost Control	
	Estimating	

EDUCATION Auburn University, Auburn, Alabama - 4 years
B.S. Degree: Industrial Management and Engineering
Major: Civil and Mechanical Engineering

EXPERIENCE
SUMMARY
1969
to Present

WELBOURNE CEMENT MANUFACTURING COMPANY
Major manufacturer of Portland Cement. Sales $165 million.

(1980
to Present)

Position: Plant Manager

Responsibilities:
-- Full responsibility for supervision and coordination of all activities in developing and implementing the plant's plans, programs and objectives.
-- Manage and direct the conversion of a 60 year old 4 million barrel cement plant to 2.5 million barrel partially automated plant; $17 million modernization program.
-- Control all operations with budgets ranging from $10 million (old plant) to $5 million (converted plant).
-- In 1980-1981 manage a new 1.25 million barrel plant with centralized control operation; $6 million budget, 85 employees.

(1977-1980)

Position; Engineer - Operations Staff, Corporate Headquarters

Responsibilities:
-- Direct all maintenance activities at 12 producing plants.
-- Monitor $8 million budget, develop maintenance control programs, training programs and cost reduction modifications.

(1971-1977)   Position: Resident Engineer

        Responsibilities:
        -- Supervise staff of engineers, inspectors and clerks in
           directing the activities of contractors in construction
           and start up of 3 new cement plants; $80 million in plant
           and related facilities construction.

(1969-1971)   Position: Field Engineer

        Responsibilities:
        -- Handle field engineering assignments as corporate repre-
           sentative, on construction projects of modernization of
           cement plants.

AVAILABILITY   6 weeks' notice required.

EMPLOYER   Present employer is not aware of decision to consider change
CONTACT   and may not be contacted at this time.

MAURICE B. LARSON

2027 Braebourne Avenue
Shawnee, OH 38276
Telephone: (812) 477-9352

OBJECTIVE <u>General Marketing Director</u>
-- Industrial Organization, marketing engineered,
   quality product lines.

SUMMARY A fully experienced marketing executive with the capability of directing an effective marketing effort through the application of experience in policy determination, sales promotion, sales administration, staff development, and sales training.

AREAS OF
KNOWLEDGE

General Marketing Management
  Organizational Structure
  Policy Determination
  Market Plan Formats
  Forecasts, 1-5 year
  Performance Appraisal
    Programs
  Market Research & Trend
    Analysis
  Merchandising, Pricing,
    Packaging

Sales Administration
  Sales Promotion, Ad-
    vertising
  Meetings, Demonstrations,
    Shows
  Sales Training, Supervi-
    sion

Product Line Development

Distribution

Dealers
Distributors
Manufacturers Agents

Engineering
  Sales
  Design
  Applications

Budget Control

<u>Markets</u>: General Industrial, marine, military; construction; farm; automotive, railroad, aircraft; refrigeration, air conditioning; materials handling, power transmission, fluid power.

<u>Products</u>: Hydraulic hose, fittings, and self-sealing couplings, mechanical rubber products (conveyor, elevator, and transmission belting, molded rubber products, and general industrial hose), cargo control products for marine, truck, and railroad industries.

EXPERIENCE
1969 to
Present

EKKOMART CORPORATION, 300 S. East Avenue, Cincinnati, OH; multi-product, multi-market industrial organization; sales volume over $100 million; 5,000 employees.

<u>Positions</u>: Marketing Manager--National Markets--following
successful promotions from:
Western Sales Manager
District Sales Manager
Account Executive

116

1977 –
Present

As Marketing Manager--National Markets

Responsibilities: The significant building of total sales volume both through the expansion of existing account business and through progressively greater market penetration

-- Direct sales administration of the national field sales force and of 6 program sales managers.

-- Supervision of Marketing Services, including personnel, new product development, market planning, field engineering, training, and advertising.

Achievements:

-- Doubled market's sales volume, from $9 million to $19 million, in 2 years.

-- Tripled profit contribution in this same period.

-- Established four market-oriented specialized sales force groups, thus accomplished above results.

-- Established successful performance appraisal programs, one and five-year marketing plans, and field training programs.

-- Effectively reorganized line-staff relationship to insure this profitable, customer-oriented growth.

1976
1977

As Western Sales Manager

Responsibilities: To accomplish major sales growth and market penetration in total area west of the Mississippi--by direct sales supervision of line sales force of district managers and field sales engineers--implementing merchandising programs and marketing plans.

Achievements:
-- Increased marine and military market penetration from $500,000 to $1,500,000 in 12 months, primarily through new product development.

-- Increased region heavy duty truck market penetration from 10% to 40%, through new product development.

-- Established selective market oriented distribution plan, replacing geographic plan, and increased aftermarket volume by 19% in one year.

117

1974 1976	<u>As District Sales Manager</u>

<u>Responsibility</u>: Sales supervision of 9 sales engineers covering industrial, OEM, distributor, and marine accounts in 5 states.

<u>Achievements</u>:
  -- Increased sales volume by <u>100%</u> in two years.

  -- Reorganized district territory layout from purely geographic to market oriented basis.

  -- Established a distributor council program that included management training. |
| 1969
1974 | <u>As Account Executive</u>, Eastern States Area

Through direct selling to marine and military accounts, built sales volume from $200,000 to $2,500,000. |
1967 1969	NEW YORK AIR BRAKE CO., Kinney Division--Sales Engineer
EDUCATION	University--Boston College Degree--B.S. in Business Administration Major--Marketing
AVAILABILITY	Within 60 days after hiring agreement.
EMPLOYER CONTACT	Present employer should not be contacted except by mutual arrangement following provisional commitment to hire.
TRAVEL	Agreeable to whatever amount is necessary to do the job--well.
LOCATE	Willing to relocate.

CAPT. WARREN JEFFERSON

PSC No. 5 Box 10842
APO San Francisco, California 96274

OBJECTIVE   Security/Law Enforcement Management

AREAS OF   Law Enforcement   Security Management
KNOWLEDGE   Air Base Police Operations   Administrative Procedures
AND   Community Patrol   Traffic Safety
EXPERIENCE   Traffic Enforcement

                 Enforcement Liaison
                 Operations Coordination   Staff Supervision
                                              Personnel
                 Community Relations   Teaching
                 Police Public Relations
                 Public Speaking   Equal Opportunity and
                                                  Treatment Practices

PERSONAL   Birthdate: 8-5-58   Married, Two children
                 5'9"   155 Lbs.   Excellent health

EDUCATION   University of Southern California, Los Angeles, Calif.
                    (1983-1985)
                    Master of Science Degree in Systems Management - 1985
                       Study Areas: Systems Analysis, Applied Statistics and
                                    Human Factors

                 Ball State University, Muncie, Indiana (1976-1980)
                    Bachelor of Science Degree in Social Science
                       Major Study Areas: Political Science, Education

                 All degree requirements completed while on active duty.

CERTIFICATION   Security Clearance: Top Secret
MEMBERSHIP   Teachers License: State of Indiana - 1980
                 International Association of Chiefs of Police

EMPLOYMENT
HISTORY
Sept., 1980   UNITED STATES AIR FORCE
to Present

                 Clark Air Force Base, Republic of the Philippines
(Sept., 1984
to Present   Position: Officer in Charge, Weapons Systems Security
                           3rd Security Police Group (Captain)

                 Responsibilities:
                 -- Manage and direct the application of the USAF weapon sys-
                    tems security program for all priority A, B and C USAF re-
                    sources (aircraft, munitions, etc.) located on Clark AF
                    Base.

119

-- Manage the development and application of security procedures for all classified operations on the base.
-- Supervise, directly and indirectly, 170 personnel.

(Oct., 1983
Sept., 1984)

Clark Air Force Base

Position: Officer in Charge, Law Enforcement Operations
          3rd Security Police Group

Responsibilities:
-- Direct and manage all law enforcement operations; base
   police operations, traffic safety and enforcement and
   town patrol operations for Clark Base and surrounding
   American community (population 29,000).
-- Maintain liaison with Philippine law enforcement officials; coordinate operations in areas of joint jurisdic-
   tion.
-- Supervise 230 personnel.

(Jan., 1982
Aug., 1983)

McChord Air Force Base, Washington

Position: C-141 Aircraft Navigator
          4th Military Airlift Squadron

Responsibilities:
-- Handle all responsibilities associated with worldwide
   navigation of C-141 transport aircraft.
-- Perform duties in all types of environment.

(Sept., 1980
Dec., 1981)

Completed undergraduate navigator training and other military
training schools.

SALARY   Open to discussion, depending on position and potential.

TRAVEL   Agreeable to any moderate amount of travel required.

LOCATION   Willing to relocate, U.S. or overseas.

AVAILABILITY   November, 1986

REFERENCES   Available upon request.

LEROY T. REDMAN

27 West Hillview St.
Bartleville, SC 28797
Telephone: (419) 712-4889

OBJECTIVE   Plant Management/Production Supervision

AREAS OF   Plant/Warehouse Management   Quality Control, Inspection
KNOWLEDGE   Product Line Development: Material/Inventory Control
AND   Design, Methods   Material Handling, Ware-
EXPERIENCE   Proficiency Techniques   house Storage
                Production Purchasing/Ex-   Shipping and Receiving
                   pediting
                Production Control,   Vendor Evaluation, Relations
                   Scheduling
                                                  Sheet Metal Fabrication
                Staff and Line Supervision   Welding Instructions
                Hiring and Training   Metal Shears, Punching,
                Employee Labor Relations   Forming Operations
                                                 Spray Painting
                Value Analysis/Engineering   Industrial, Commercial
                Time and Motion Evaluation
                Systems and Procedures
                Feasibility Studies

SPECIAL   American Association of Industrial Management courses.
TRAINING

EXPERIENCE
1981 to   HANNSEN FIREPROOF DOOR CO., Bartleville, SC
Present   Sheet metal fabrication, hollow metal doors and frames. An-
                nual sales volume $8.5 million.

                Position: Plant Manager

                Reponsibilities:
                  -- Supervise plant operations: shearing, punching, forming,
                     spot welding, welding, assembly, finish grinding, paint-
                     ing, shipping, receiving, maintenance, quality control.
                  -- Handle production planning and control; develop new pro-
                     duction methods.
                  -- Develop new prototypes and techniques.
                  -- Direct personnel: hire, train, supervise; handle union-
                     labor relations; maintain time cards and cost of labor.
                  -- Handle ordering and expediting of production supplies.

Achievements:
-- Expanded total production from $43,000 to $89,000 per week in a 3-year period.
-- Achieved 40 - 50% increase in plant efficiency.
-- In a 6-month period, reduced overtime from an average of 16 hours to 2 hours per week per person, while increasing production 25% with 10% fewer people.
-- Reduced backlog from 12 weeks to 8 weeks.
-- Reduced indirect-to-direct labor ratio from 15% to 2%.

1978
1981

CORDA CORPORATION, Summit, SC
Light manufacturing and packaging of scuba equipment. Annual sales volume $6 million.

Position: Plant Superintendent.

Responsibilities:
-- Direct all plant operations, including assembly of precision gauges and regulators: production schedules, warehouse layout and storage, quality control and inspection, personnel.
-- Handle new tool and prototype development; improve packaging.

Achievements:
-- Achieved more than 100% increase in plant efficiency.
-- Reduced production costs 40% - 100% by immediately converting all raw stock into shippable merchandise, thereby eliminating warehousing and the problem of back ordering.
-- Successfully managed a stock project costing over $250,000; resulted in substantial annual savings in operating cost and time.
-- Made layout improvements which utilized existing area to increase shipping and receiving by 55%; reduced indirect labor 30% through new product line design and location.

1974
1978

GENERAL BLOWER CORPORATION, Wheeling, Illinois
Sheet metal fabrication; commercial and industrial air moving equipment. Annual sales volume $2 million.

Position: Foreman

Responsibilities:
-- Manage the warehouse.
-- Responsible for sheet metal fabrication operations: line supervision, proficiency techniques, value analysis and value engineering, time and motion evaluation, quality control, inspection.
-- Supervise training: assembly, welding, painting.
-- Handle vendor evaluation/relations and employer labor relations.

MARK L. O'FALLON

2211 North Belvidere
Buffalo Grove, IL 60009
Telephone: (312) 396-4469

OBJECTIVE   <u>Plant Management/Production Control</u>

SUMMARY   A Plant and Production Management man with solid experience,
            broad background and a demonstrated ability to increase pro-
            fits through manufacturing improvements.

AREAS OF   Plant Management   Quality Control
KNOWLEDGE   Production Scheduling   Purchasing
            Cost Calculations
            Cost Estimating   Labor Relations
                                          Union Negotiations
            Plant Engineering
            Troubleshooting   Supervision
                                          Hiring, Training
            Production Control   Rates and Wage Incentive
            Inventory Control   System
            Material Control

EDUCATION   Pennsylvania Military College, Chester, Pa.
              Evening Division: 2 yrs.
                Major: Chemistry

EXPERIENCE
1982 to   MEDIUM SIZE MANUFACTURER OF DENTAL MATERIALS, Chicago area.
Present   Annual sales $5 million.

            Position: Plant/Production Manager

            Responsibilities:
              -- Direct and manage all manufacturing operations, with full
                 responsibility for quality and quantity of production.
              -- Coordinate activities of various plant departments; produc-
                 tion engineering, quality control, purchasing, production
                 control, inventory.
              -- Control the maintenance of all equipment.

            Achievements:
              -- Increased production output in one Department by 80% with
                 only a 20% increase in direct labor, by redesigning the
                 process equipment.
              -- Established an effective inventory control system for raw
                 materials and packaging items.

123

| 1976 | MAJOR PLASTICS, INC., CHICAGO. Manufacturer of vinyl heat |
| 1982 | sealing products. Sales volume $3.5 million. |

Position: Production Control

Responsibilities:
-- Manage the production of vinyl heat sealed products utilizing high frequency electronic equipment, vinyl die cutting beam presses, slitters, routing machines, button at-
   tachers and single and multi colored silk screening process.
-- Prepare cost analysis reports; bid competitively on new
   work.
-- Supervise 5 salaried and 60 hourly employees.
-- Maintain and build good customer relations.

Achievements:
-- Established and then maintained production standards.
-- Set up an improved production and inventory control, which
   smoothed production and assured accurate physical inven-
   tory and records.
-- Improved stockroom layout; reduced double handling.

| 1964 | ESSCHEM COMPANY, Essington, Pennsylvania. Manufacturers of |
| 1976 | chemicals and dental acrylics. Sales volume $5 million. |

(1973-1976)   Position: Production Manager

Earnings: $13,000 salary plus bonus and stock options.

Responsibilities:
-- Directly responsible for the manufacturing of dental acry-
   lics.
-- Coordinate all departments to insure even work flow.
-- Maintain liaison and communications with sales and service
   departments.

Achievements:
-- Arranged to handle up to a 30% greater work volume and
   still maintained an even flow of production.
-- Tested, adapted and installed new machinery which increased
   production and reduced costs.

(1969-1973)   Position: Production Manager

Responsibilities:
-- Direct all activities of the Maintenance Department.
-- Secure bids from contractors for plant expansion programs;
   purchase new equipment and replacement parts.
-- Supervise 5 maintenance employees.

(1964-1969)   Position: Plant Engineer

EMPLOYER   Present employer is not aware of decision to consider change
CONTACT   and may not be contacted at this time.

MERLE CANTRELL

10721 Allegheny Road
Pittsburgh, PA 18941
Telephone: (213) 420-2022

OBJECTIVE   Project Engineer Management

SUMMARY   An experienced Project Engineer with a solid background of
                 performance. Resourceful in handling problems--and equipped
                 by explicit, pertinent experience to be of immediate value.

EDUCATION   University of Notre Dame, Notre Dame, Indiana
                     B.S. Degree - Aeronautical Engineering - 1957
                 Fellowship, Industrial Hygiene Foundation, Mellon Institute,
                     Pittsburgh, Pa. Environmental studies.

PROFESSIONAL   Registered Professional Engineer - State of Pennsylvania
STATUS AND   Association of Iron and Steel Engineers
MEMBERSHIPS   Air Pollution Control Association

EXPERIENCE
1957 to   THE NATIONAL STEEL CORPORATION
Present

(1979 to   Position: Project Engineer, Central Design Office
Present)
                 Responsibilities: Coordinate design to complete: (a) $40
                 million bar mill; (b) $5 million pollution control equipment
                 for an Electric Furnace Shop; (c) $3 million air pollution
                 control facility for an Iron Ore Sintering Plant.

                 Reason to Change: National engineering facility being moved to
                 New Jersey; family decision not to relocate there.

(1977-1979)   Position: Supervisor of Project Engineering

                 Responsibilities: Attended Company Engineering Management
                 Training Course; supervised the development of the North Works
                 appropriation budget and prepared the plant's long-range plan.

(1974-1977)   Position: Supervisor of Project Engineering - Steel Production
                           Division

                 Responsibilities:
                 -- Developed layout for North Works oxygen steel making faci-
                    lity; after Management approval, acted as liaison with
                    Pittsburgh Engineering Office until the project was com-
                    pleted.
                 -- Engineered and installed two $1 million projects; pressure
                    casting of steel and vacuum degassing of steel.
                 -- Supervised 2 Design Engineers and 13 Draftsmen.

125

(1964-1973)   Position: Power and Fuel Engineer, after promotion from De-
                             sign Engineer

                   Responsibilities: (1968-1973)
                   -- Heating and ventilating two rolling mill electrical motor
                      rooms; piping and mechanical services design for a plant
                      chemical laboratory ($700,000); full project responsibility
                      for facilities to house IBM computer equipment; redesigned
                      "in plant" environmental control equipment for an iron ore
                      sintering machine -- was awarded a patent and approval for
                      implementing the $750,000 project.
                   -- Represented North Works as Technical Advisor on air pollu-
                      tion; served on the Mayor's industrial committee to write
                      Air Pollution code and the Association of Commerce and In-
                      dustry committee for Zoning Ordinance.

                   Responsibilities:
                   -- Supervised the detailed design of 2 steam turbine driven
                      air compressors for Blast Furnace blowing ($4 million);
                      supervised the installation; project engineer for installa-
                      tion of 70 ton per day oxygen generation plant.

(1957-1963)   Position: Engineer (Power and Fuel) after promotion from
                             Trainee.

                   Responsibilities: Steam power plant engineering and utility
                   distribution piping design; calculations, sketches, specifica-
                   tions, review of final drawings; review and approval of boilers
                   up to 600,000 pounds per hour, 900 psig.

TRAVEL   Agreeable to any amount required by the position.

LOCATE   Prefer to remain in the Pittsburgh area.

EMPLOYER   Present employer may be contacted at any time.
CONTACT

REFERENCES   References are available immediately upon request.

MICHAEL R. BRIDGER

14950 Bothel Drive
Seattle, WA 98107
Telephone: (206) 391-0457

OBJECTIVE

Project Manufacturing Engineering Management: Plastics

HIGHLIGHTS
OF
BACKGROUND

* Successfully handled a number of $500,000 tooling programs from the initial tool and part cost estimate to full production.
* Designed and wrote a training program for basic mold design, which was used personally in Japan for instruction to Harper & Todd employees there.
* Recommended the use of alternate plastic materials; recommendation accepted and Company saved over $80,000 per year.
* Supervised press installations and molding operation start up in Japan.
* Developed a preventive maintenance program to assure part supply for high production (camera) assembly line.
* Supervised the set up and start up of injection molding operation for closures; production increased from 1,000 to 6,000 closures per month in 14 months.
* Successfully managed all phases of a (6 press) injection molding operation and maintained a 94% machine utilization.
* Directed the initial use and development of a low cost, quick change "Master Unit Die" system.
* Designed and developed a "quick screen change mechanism" for high production plastic resin extruders. Patent issued.

AREAS OF
KNOWLEDGE
AND
EXPERIENCE

Project Engineering
Mechanical Engineering
Production Engineering

Mold Design
Moldmaking

Production Start Up
Troubleshooting
Cost Reduction

Training/Teaching
Group Supervision (Tool
    Process Engineering)

Product Cost Analysis
Timing and Scheduling
Material Specifications
Purchasing

Computerized Process Control
Quality Assurance
Extruder - Screw and Die
    Head Design

Foreign Relations/Liaison
Foreign Languages
Long Range Planning

127

EDUCATION	Bundes Gewerbeschule, Bilz, Austria
	   (Mechanical - Electrical Engineering)
	      Engineering Graduate
	Special Training Courses:
	   Geometric Dimensioning and Tolerancing

EXPERIENCE

Aug., 1976 Aug., 1986	HARPER & TODD, Seattle, WA Manufacturer of photo products. Annual sales $100 million; 1,000 employees.

(May, 1981
Aug., 1986)
	<u>Position</u>: Project Manufacturing Engineer, Plastics
	
	<u>Responsibilities</u>:
	-- Overall responsibility for applying a full range of know-
	   ledge and principles to involved projects.
	-- Assist in the establishment of product specifications.
	-- Make feasibility and manufacturing cost studies for major
	   projects.
	-- Supervise the work (in-house or purchased) of tool de-
	   signers, engineers and developers, as required to complete
	   an assigned project.

(Aug., 1976 May, 1981)	<u>Position</u>: Senior Manufacturing Engineer <u>Responsibilities</u>: -- Responsibilities and assignments basically the same as above.

Feb., 1975
Aug., 1976
	BURNS PLASTIC, Palatine, Illinois
	Custom molder closures; annual sales volume $600,000; 80
	employees.
	
	<u>Position</u>: Vice President of Manufacturing, after promotion
	           from Plant Engineer
	
	<u>Responsibilities</u>:
	-- Overall responsibility for all manufacturing.
	   Plant layout
	   Machine set up/construction set up
	   Tool estimate
	   Design; development
	   Production output
	   Operator and moldmaker training

1971 1975	FEDERAL TOOL AND PLASTICS, Chicago, Illinois Manufacturer of housewares and custom molder. <u>Positions</u>: Mold Designer and Developer, after promotion from Moldmaker

Responsibilities:
-- Mold design, development and construction.
-- Cost estimates.

1969
1971

WERNER AND PFLEIDERER, Stuttgart, West Germany.
Machine builder.

Position: Mechanical Design Engineer

Responsibilities:
-- Design and test extrusion die heads and put them into
   production at customer plant.

1965
1969

THERMOPLAST COMPANY, Linz, Austria
Custom molder.

Position: Lead Moldmaker, after promotion from Moldmaker.

SALARY   Open to discussion, depending on position and potential.

TRAVEL   Agreeable to any occasional travel necessary.

LOCATE   Willing to relocate.

AVAILABILITY   30-60 days' notice required.

EMPLOYER   Present employer is not aware of decision to consider change
CONTACT   and may not be contacted at this time.

REFERENCES   References available upon request.

FOREIGN   Fluent in German and English
LANGUAGE

FOREIGN   Business trips to Japan, Portugal, Spain, Italy, England and
TRAVEL   Germany.

JUDITH MYERS GREY

4313 South Harper
Chicago, IL 60616
Telephone: (312) 633-8381

OBJECTIVE   <u>Senior Level Administration: Public Affairs</u>
         -- Government or Business and Industry

AREAS OF   General Administration   Public Administration
KNOWLEDGE   Policy Formation   Legislative and Policy
            Organizational Structure   Research
              and Development   Federal Grants-in-Aid
                                            Grant Application Drafting
            Operating Procedures
            Program Planning and   Community Organization
              Evaluation
            Budget Development   State and Local Governments:
                                        Function and Structure
            Report Drafting, Editing   Public Relations

EDUCATION   University of Chicago, Chicago, Illinois
             M.A. Degree - 1980
           Mankato State College, Mankato, Minnesota
             B.A. Degree - 1973
             Major: Political Science   Minors: History, English
           Special Training: Graduate work in the social sciences; empha-
             sis on policy development in government and economics.

PROFESSIONAL   The American Academy of Political and Social Science
ACTIVITY   Center for the Study of Democratic Institutions

EXPERIENCE
July, 1981   GOVERNOR'S OFFICE OF HUMAN RESOURCES, STATE OF ILLINOIS,
June, 1986   Chicago, Illinois.

            <u>Position</u>: Director of Program Development

            <u>Responsibilities</u>:
             -- Plan, evaluate and coordinate a broad range of Federal,
                State and local programs with emphasis on health, dan-
                gerous drugs, employment and community assistance.
             -- Administer a staff of 10 professionals and 5 clerical
                personnel, with an annual budget of $250,000.

Achievements:
-- Substantially increased the effectiveness of the Illinois
   Drug Abuse Program by securing a grant of $220,000.
-- Directed a comprehensive analysis of the Amendments to the
   Social Security Act (HR-1); results of analysis incor-
   porated by Illinois Governor in his presentation to the
   U.S. Congress.
-- A study of Illinois' nutrition programs, along with legis-
   lative and administrative recommendations, had a major im-
   pact on Senator Charles Percy's subcommittee on Nutrition
   and Health.
-- Initiated and implemented the Governor's Conference on
   Women's Rights.

Aug., 1979   COMMISSION OF URBAN AREA GOVERNMENT, STATE OF ILLINOIS,
June, 1981   Chicago, Illinois.

Position: Assistant Director

Responsibilities and Achievements:
-- Serve as Secretary to Executive Committee; maintain liaison with Regional committees.
-- Establish and conduct public hearings on matters affecting
   state-local government in context of statutory and constitutional revision.
-- Organize Regional committees to study state-local problems
   in Illinois' major cities.
-- Draft and edit reports and recommendations based on research and data supplied by the Committee and public
   groups.
-- Develop recommendations on local government for the Illinois Constitutional Convention; report and recommendations to the Convention were essentially incorporated into
   the new Constitution and instrumental in its approval by
   referendum.

Oct., 1977   EDUCATIONAL DEVELOPMENT COOPERATIVE, Homewood, Ill.
Oct., 1978   Non-profit public corporation of 60 Cook County school dis-
               tricts.

Responsibilities and Achievements:
-- Advise and represent the Superintendents of the 67 subur-
   ban Cook County school districts on matters of State and
   Federal legislation and programs.
-- Planned and coordinated a 3-day conference in Washington,
   D.C., for the Cooperative membership; meetings with the
   Secretary and staff of U.S. Office of Education and with
   members of Congressional education committees.

Reason for Change: Entered University of Chicago graduate
school to earn Masters Degree.

Sept., 1976 EXECUTIVE OFFICE OF THE GOVERNOR, STATE OF IOWA, Des Moines,
Oct., 1977   Iowa.

Position: Deputy Director of the Office of Economic Opportunity.

Responsibilities and Achievements:
-- Brief the Governor on Federal grant applications to the Office of Economic Opportunity.
-- Act as Consultant on organizational and administrative matters to Community Action Agencies in Iowa's major cities.
-- Solve problems as intermediary between Federal and local officials and administrators.
-- Personal efforts resulted in successful establishment of Community Action Agencies in Iowa's 7 largest urban areas.

July, 1975   POLK COUNTY COMMUNITY ACTION COUNCIL, Des Moines, Iowa
Sept., 1976

Position: Assistant Director

Responsibilities and Achievements:
-- Organize neighborhood and community groups; secure contributions of funds and equipment.
-- Establish liaison with private and public service agencies.
-- Handle public relations; draft grant applications.
-- Conduct demographic and economic research.
-- Successfully set up a viable Community Action Agency in Iowa's largest metropolitan area, with a $1 million budget; accomplished within one year by a 3-man staff.
-- Established numerous effective community organizations where none had previously existed.

June, 1974   IOWA LEGISLATIVE RESEARCH BUREAU, STATE OF IOWA, Des Moines,
July, 1975   Iowa.

Position: Research Analyst

Responsibilities: Research analysis of statutes; draft and proof legislative bills. Provide legislative information/data to legislators. Secretary to legislative committees.

MILTON F. TOBIN

2417 Parkway Drive
Northfield, MN 51412
Telephone: (612) 411-7019

OBJECTIVE   Director of Purchasing

AREAS OF   Purchasing Management   Negotiation
KNOWLEDGE   Departmental Administration   Contracts
                   Purchasing Policy Development
                   Purchasing Systems and   Material Handling, Storage
                       Procedures   Product Analysis
                                                      Materials Changes
                   Vendor Evaluation, Selection
                   Vendor Relations   Purchasing Quantity Control
                                                      Purchasing Timing Control
                   Expediting
                   Coordinating   Staff Supervision
                   Problem Solving   Employment, Training

                   Blanket Order Purchasing

PRODUCT AND   Cosmetics and Toiletries   MRO and Office Supplies
RAW MATERIAL   Pharmaceuticals   Machinery
EXPERIENCE   Food Manufacture
                   Environmental Cleaning and
                       Waxes

PROFESSIONAL   Purchasing Management Association of Minneapolis/St. Paul
MEMBERSHIPS   American Association of Industrial Management

EXPERIENCE
1974 to   LARGE DIVERSIFIED MANUFACTURER OF FOOD, TOILETRIES,
Present   PHARMACEUTICALS. Annual sales volume over $100 million.

                   Position: Manager, Raw Material and MRO Purchases, after pro-
                             motions from Senior Buyer and Buyer

                   Responsibilities:
                   -- To direct, supervise and coordinate purchases of raw ma-
                      terials and MRO for 4 Divisions.
                   -- To be responsible for all inventories.
                   -- To supervise the activities of 4 Buyers, including train-
                      ing.
                   -- To personally participate in purchasing activities: analyze
                      requisitions, contact vendors, interview salesmen, review
                      and approve sources, long term contracts and blanket orders.

133

Achievements:
-- Effected departmental savings of at least $250,000 per year for 5 years.
-- Personally accomplished direct savings of $100,000 in last 2 years.
-- Designed and placed blanket orders which accomplished yearly savings of $50,000.
-- Negotiated a 25% price reduction in Tomato Paste which saved $37,500 in 1980.
-- Reduced inventory investment by $300,000 by establishing a stocking source and eliminating a 3-week lead time.
-- Accomplished a scrap disposal income of $15,000 per year.
-- Tightened inventory control to a 3 weeks supply level and increased turnover from 6 to 12 times per year.
-- Profitably developed vendor and purchase bases changes.
-- Profitably developed materials changes.

1964
1974

JULIAN LABORATORIES, Minneapolis, Minnesota. Pharmaceutical manufacturer. Annual sales volume approximately $9 million.

Position: Purchasing Agent

Responsibilities:
-- To coordinate activities of purchasing and movement of production materials, capital equipment, maintenance and supplies.
-- To supervise production scheduling, inventory control, shipping and receiving.
-- To establish basic policies and systems for purchasing and materials controls.
-- To be responsible for vendor relations.
-- To analyze markets to determine present and future availability and price trends.

Achievements:
-- Installed a successful inventory control system; saved $20,000 annually through purchase item card system with min-max amounts, order points, order amounts.
-- Saved $85,000 a year by installation of bulk solvent system.
-- Set up a recirculating condenser water system which reduced operating costs by $10,000 a year.
-- Originated effective quality control and timing control systems.

1960
1964

THE GLIDDEN COMPANY, SOYA PRODUCTS DIVISION, Chicago, Illinois. Paint and pharmaceutical manufacturer. Annual sales volume $110 million.

Position: Buyer, after promotion from Chemist.

PETER F. PLANTE

2170 Surrey Lane
Columbus, OH 40021
Telephone: (389) 375-3217

OBJECTIVE   Senior Management: Quality Assurance

HIGHLIGHTS   As Director of Quality Assurance and Technical Service
OF QUALITY   .. Directed activity resulting in $750,000 (annualized) sav-
ASSURANCE   ings in cost improvement projects (1985).
CAREER   .. Reduced percent defective in adhesive bandages from 13% to
                      1% in 2 years.
                   .. Reduced customer complaints in hospital tape from 20 per
                      month to 5 per quarter (1985).
                   .. Conducted successful FDA inspection in 1985.
                   .. Instrumental in having a subordinate promoted to Director of
                      Quality Assurance for another Company plant.

                   As Group Manager of Quality Assurance and Technical Service
                   .. Established very effective vendor audit program.
                   .. Revised and improved inspection procedures to deal with in-
                      creasing customer complaints.
                   .. Set up sampling plan in baby products to assure compliance
                      with label claim regulations.
                   .. Through period of raw material shortage, maintained the busi-
                      ness without compromising the quality of products.
                   .. Established essential microbial impound area for toiletries.

                   As Manager of Quality Assurance
                   .. Improved in-process procedures for handling prescription
                      items.
                   .. Established overtime and promotion policies which resolved a
                      difficult employee relations problem.

                   As Group Leader - Technical Service
                   .. Saved $600,000 (annualized) in cost improvement projects.
                   .. Coordinated successful pollution abatement project.

                   As Technical Service Scientist
                   .. Resolved vinyl casting process problem: changed operation
                      from $250,000 loss (1980) to a $350,000 gain (1981).

PERSONAL   Birthdate: 2-4-53   Married, Two children
                   5'11"   175 Lbs.   Excellent Health

EDUCATION   Ohio State University, Columbus, OH
                     MBA Degree - 1983   Major: Finance
                     B.S. Degree - 1975
                       Major: Biology   Minor: Chemistry

PROFESSIONAL   American Society for Quality Control
MEMBERSHIPS   American Chemical Society: Rubber Division
                   Society of Plastics Engineers

135

AREAS OF KNOWLEDGE AND EXPERIENCE	Quality Assurance Management	Resources Planning
	Statistical Quality Control	Manpower Planning
	Government Regulations	
	FDA Inspections	Affirmative Action
	Quality Improvement Programs	Employee Relations
	Technical Service Management	Customer Relations
	Specifications	
	Government Contracts	Sterilization
	Systems, Procedures	Rubber, Gauze, Fibre,
	Cost Improvement Programs	Plastics and Adhesive Processing
	Budgets	
	Financial Reporting	Health Care Industry
	Standard Cost Systems	

EXPERIENCE SUMMARY
Sept., 1980 to Present

LEADING MANUFACTURER OF HEALTH CARE PRODUCTS
Manufacture and distribution of health care products. $2 billion total company sales volume.

(June, 1985 to Present)

Position: Director of Quality Assurance and Technical Service
Report to National Director in New Jersey

Responsibilities:
-- Manage Quality Assurance, Analytical and Microbiological Laboratories, and Technical Service functions for Company's 2 Ohio plants; $80 million sales volume, 1800 employees.
-- Control a $2 million budget; establish local policy and implement national policy.
-- Direct short and long range planning.
-- Maintain communications with senior management of all Divisions as well as Headquarters.
-- Supervise subordinate managerial, scientific and technical personnel; total staff of 115.

Reason to Change: Family decision not to relocate to Northeastern United States.

(Aug., 1983 June, 1985)

Position: Group Manager of Quality Assurance and Technical Service.

Responsibilities:
-- Manage Quality Assurance and Technical Service areas for Baby Products and Surgical Adhesive Mill, and Distribution Center; $750,000 budget; staff of 50.
-- Approve specifications and test methods.
-- Resolve quality problems.
-- Hire and train employees; manage salary administration.

(Feb., 1983 Aug., 1983)	Position: Manager of Quality Assurance Responsibilities: -- Responsibilities of Quality Assurance for gauze and fibre products, basically the same in principle as the above positions; review product quality monthly with manufactur-ing management.
(Sept., 1981 Feb., 1983)	Position: Group Leader - Technical Service Responsibilities: -- Direct project activities for gauze, fibre and adhesive mills; maintenance, cost reduction, purchasing. -- Handle new product development and specification changes.
(Sept., 1980 Sept., 1981)	Position: Technical Service Scientist - Surgical Adhesive Mill Responsibilities: -- Product and process maintenance; new product introduction, purchasing support, quality improvement.
Sept., 1975 Sept., 1980	SAMUEL BINGHAM COMPANY, Franklin Park, Illinois. Industrial rubber products; sales volume $10 million.
(Sept., 1979 Sept., 1980)	Position: Technical Service Manager Responsibilities and Achievements: -- Overall responsibility for in-house quality assurance and technical service to customers in 15 states. -- Saved substantial number of accounts from cancelling orders. Prior Positions: Technical Service (9/77 - 9/79) R & D Chemist (9/75 - 9/77)
TRAVEL	Agreeable as required -- up to 50%
LOCATION	Willing to relocate.
AVAILABILITY	30 days' notice required.
EMPLOYER CONTACT	Present employer is not aware of decision to consider change and may not be contacted at this time.
REFERENCES	Available upon request.

JERRY PIKE

207 Central Park West
New York, NY 02198
Telephone: (212) 935-1717

OBJECTIVE   Real Estate: Senior Administrative Position
                   -- Management, Appraisals, Investment Analysis, Per-
                      sonnel Training
                   -- Apartment Buildings, Commercial, Industrial and
                      Shopping Centers

PROFESSIONAL   National Association of Real Estate Boards
MEMBERSHIPS,   National Association of Ind. Fee Appraisers
ACTIVITIES   International Real Estate Federation
                   International Traders Club
                   National Association of Farm and Land Brokers
                   Eastern Real Estate Board
                   North Side Real Estate Board

                   Executive positions with various Real Estate Boards
                   Chairman and member: Real Estate Board Committees:
                        Appraisal, Cooperative Listing, Ethics, Membership,
                        Management, Traders, Sales Awards
                   Guest Speaker: most major State Real Estate Boards
                   Guest Lecturer: Dale Carnegie Course

PUBLICATIONS   Numerous published articles on investments, syndications and
                   sale leasebacks for trade publications and newspapers.

EXPERIENCE
1980 to   MAJOR REAL ESTATE MANAGEMENT FIRM
Present
                   Position: Vice President, Assistant Director of Management

                   Responsibilities:
                   -- Active management of 675,000 sq. ft. of multitenant in-
                      dustrial spaces, 7 local retail shopping strips comprising
                      46 retail tenants and 1200 apartment units.

                   Achievements:
                   -- Reduced industrial vacancy from 18% to 0; increased rentals
                      to cover cost increases.
                   -- Redesigned heating systems to effect substantial savings.
                   -- Re-leased prime units to major national tenants.
                   -- Revised all renewals to compensate for inflationary in-
                      creases.
                   -- Produced a higher net cash flow for all management units.
                   -- Tightened personnel activities, reduced labor costs and in-
                      creased services.

1975
1980 MANHATTAN REAL ESTATE
Real Estate management, sales, investment, appraisals.

Position: General Manager

Responsibilities;
-- Developed active real estate operation involving investment, general brokerage, management and appraisal services.
-- Hired and trained staff of 15 full time professional investment consultants.
-- Managed 960 apartment rental units and varied commercial
properties.

Achievements:
-- Personally developed, sold and syndicated investment properties. Sold Outer Drive East Apartments (Sale Leaseback),
400 West Randolph, 1976. Largest brokerage deal in history
of the Company.
-- Developed marketing oriented techniques for sub-average va-
cancy controls; introduced tenant motivation procedures.
-- Initiated automated bookkeeping systems to produce total
informative daily reports.
-- Drastically reduced contract maintenance.
-- Modified leases and procedures to assure full lessor agent
unit controls.

1969
1974 J. KRUGER & CO., REALTORS, Chicago

Position: Partner

Achievements:
-- Provided leadership and management to the firm, which con-
tributed substantially to a volume increase from under $9
million to over $39 million.
-- Expanded firm's activities from 1 salesman to 38 Asso-
ciates; 1 office to 3 covering Chicago, the North Shore and
Northwest suburbs.
-- First year: hired and trained 12 Associates, built sales up
to $2.8 million.
-- As a 50% Partner, developed a Management Division which ac-
quired almost 700 units; created and supervised separate
Investment and Acquisition Divisions.

1968
1969 BALDWIN & ASSOCIATES, Chicago.
Real estate development and investment.

Position: Director of Developments

Achievements:
-- Coordinated new construction development programs and management system.
-- Directed investment financing and syndication programs.
-- Rejuvenated staff with new personnel and training programs.

1962
1967

MONTGOMERY & KIRSCHNER, REALTORS, INC., Chicago

Position; Director of Sales and Developments

Responsibilities:
-- Created and consummated first large scale trading programs of investment.
-- Wrote all contracts; arranged financing and closed all transactions; hired and trained new staff.

Achievements:
-- Successfully consummated a complex multi-unit investment trade, involving five separate parcels scattered throughout Chicago and suburbs; encompassed 6 principals, 8 attorneys, 4 cooperating brokers; required 2 days rehearsing for closing at C.T.& T.; value $9.2 million.
-- Accepted and actively served on committee as Consultant for local Ward, on development of then new Chicago Comprehensive Zoning Plan.
-- Became founding member of Cooperative Listing Service of North Shore Real Estate Board; Service grew from 12 members to one of largest in the United States, with 160 member offices and 1250 salesmen.
-- Designed and conducted Investment, Sales and Trading courses for the Cooperative Listing Service.

AVAILABILITY   Immediate

REFERENCES   Business and personal references available upon request.

MARY HOLMES
9121 West Broadlawn
Bangor, ME 06921
Telephone: (286) 479-6743

OBJECTIVE   <u>Store Manager/Assistant Store Manager/Floor Manager</u>

Retail Merchandising

AREAS OF
KNOWLEDGE
AND
EXPERIENCE

Store Management	Customer/Public Relations
Department Management	
Full Profit Responsibility	Staff Meetings
Sales	Staff Supervision
	Personnel Hiring, Development
Payroll Control	
Expense Control	Office Management
Inventory Control	
Shrinkage Control	Warehouse Management
Purchasing/Pricing	Material Handling
	Routing, Tracing, Expediting
Advertising	Trucking
Special Promotions	

EXPERIENCE
1979
Present

E. J. KORVETTE - NORTHEAST DIVISION. Nationwide retail store
Chain. Annual sales volume: Oldtower - $12 million; Waterville
Falls - $8 million.

<u>Position</u>; Department Manager - Linens and Domestics (1 year)
Shoes (8 years)

Responsibilities:
-- Total responsibility for management, operation, merchan-
   dising and purchasing for the Department.
-- Create and develop weekly advertising plus special promo-
   tions to build sales.
-- Control expenses, payroll, inventory and mark-downs.
-- Develop good Company image among customers.
-- Train new management personnel for other stores in the
   chain.

Achievements:
-- Received recognition as one of the top Department Managers
   in the chain; top Departmental Manager in total sales in
   Linens and Shoe Department among all 12 stores in Northeast
   Division.
-- Remodeled and reset both Departments for better traffic
   flow.
-- Reduced shrinkage in Linen Dept. by 5% of sales in 2 years.
-- Recognized as a competent trainer and developer of people;
   trained over 20 new management individuals for other stores
   in Maine.

SCOUNT STORES, Chicago, Illinois
self-service chain. Annual sales volume $2 million.

on: Store Manager

nsibilities:
otal profit responsibility and direction of entire store
operations.
Responsible for proper handling of all revenue and dis-
bursements, requisitioning of new stocks, inventory control, sales and sales promotions, supervision of employees,
records and reports, and cost control.
-- Maintain close control of expenses, with special emphasis
on payroll.

Achievements:
-- Successfully and profitably managed the top store in the
chain, with $400,000 sales volume.
-- Increased sales in all 3 stores managed.
-- Received recognition as "the outstanding store manager" in
the chain.
-- Maintained above-average units both customer relation-wise
and cleanliness-wise.
-- Trained new management personnel for other stores in the
chain.

PERSONAL	Birthdate: 8-6-50	Single
	5'4" 125 Lbs.	Excellent Health
SALARY	Open to discussion, depending on position and potential.	
TRAVEL	Agreeable to any moderate amount of travel required.	
LOCATION	Prefer the New England area.	
AVAILABILITY	3-4 weeks' notice required.	
EMPLOYER CONTACT	Present employer is not aware of decision to consider change and may not be contacted at this time.	
REFERENCES	Available upon request.	

CLIFFORD L. MARSTON

871 Bayside Terrace
Tulsa, OK 41971
Telephone: (512) 629-0272

OBJECTIVE   Sales, Leading to Sales Management
                  -- Industrial Products

HIGHLIGHTS   As Sales Representative: Industrial Rubber Distribu...
OF SALES   .. Increased territory sales at least 200% during last 2 years
CAREER   by increasing diversification of product base.
                .. Increased Key Account sales approximately 20%.
                .. Made substantial improvement in collections; all accounts
                   now reduced to an average of 25 days with none exceeding 60
                   days.

             As District Manager, Salesman: Boston Industrial Products
                .. Obtained 2 million foot hose order from key target OEM not
                   previously sold by the Company; value of order, $110,000.
                .. Obtained $21,000 conveyor belt order from one new account.
                .. Added new hose distributor; 9-month purchases amounted to
                   $60,000.
                .. Increased total sales by 70% during 9 months.
                .. Broadened the products purchased by accounts.

             As District Manager, Salesman: Dayco Corporation
                .. Added 40 new distributors; increased sales from $300,000
                   to $750,000.
                .. Accomplished a 40% reduction in warehouse inventory while
                   sales were increasing, with no hardship to customers.
                .. Handled the introduction of the safety lawn mower blade for
                   sale through True Value, Walgreen, and Osco.
                .. Set up special program for sale of farm market hydraulic
                   hose and couplings to Cotter & Co. (True Value Hardware
                   Stores).
                .. Increased sales sufficiently to necessitate the creation
                   of a new territory between Indianapolis and Chicago.
                .. Established distributor sales program with costs split be-
                   tween the Company and distributor; program still being used.

AREAS OF   OEM Sales   Warehouse Inventory Control
KNOWLEDGE   Distributor Set-up/Contact/
AND   Control   Territory Layout
EXPERIENCE   Consumer Sales   Sales Incentive Program
             Key Accounts   Compensation Plans
                                            Sales Training - Distributor
             Special Product Marketing   Sales

             Sales Forecasting and Budgets Trade Shows

143

Birthdate: 8-23-50   Married, Two children
5'8"   160 Lbs.   Excellent Health

Sept., 1983   SYBTECH CORPORATION, Tulsa, OK.
to Present   Industrial rubber distributor. Annual sales volume $4 million.

Position: Sales Representative

Responsibilities:
-- Solicit and obtain sales of O rings and seals, mechanical
   power transmission equipment and hose (metal and rubber)
   from OEM and consumer accounts in the Oklahoma and Texas
   area.
-- Responsible for semi-retired President's key accounts:
   day-to-day activities and yearly blanket purchases.
-- Handle all house accounts and related problems: sales and
   collections.

Dec., 1982   BOSTON INDUSTRIAL PRODUCTS DIVISION, American Biltrite Rubber
Sept., 1983   Company, Broadview, Illinois. Manufacturer of rubber products.

Position: District Manager, Salesman

Responsibilities:
-- Handle sales to OEM accounts.
-- Make distributor sales in northwest Indiana, northern Il-
   linois, and edge of Iowa; build and maintain good relations.
-- Introduce new products through established distributors;
   secure new distributors.
-- Train distributor salesmen through joint calls and sales
   meetings.

Dec., 1977   DAYCO CORPORATION, Franklin Park, Illinois.
Dec., 1982   Manufacturer of rubber products.

Position: District Manager, Salesman

Responsibilities:
-- Sell to OEM and distributor accounts in northwest Indiana,
   northern Illinois and edge of Iowa.
-- Manage sub-warehouse with $400,000 inventory-distributor
   cost.
-- Manage product sales through 90 distributors; maintain
   good relations.
-- Conduct educational product seminars for distributors and
   their customers.
-- Establish sound financial understanding between the Company
   and its customers.

144

| June, 1975 | GATES RUBBER COMPANY, Denver, Colorado. |
| Dec., 1977 | |

(Dec., 1976
Dec., 1977)

Position: Sales Engineer

Responsibilities:
-- Sell to Metropolitan Detroit area industrial distributors
   and OEMs: Ford Tractor, Massey Ferguson.
-- Work with distributor sales force to increase volume of
   consumer business.

(June, 1975
Dec., 1976)

Position: Sales Service Engineer

Responsibilities:
-- Supplement the Chicago based salesmen through added
   coverage of industrial distributors.
-- Resolve problems concerning billing, special allowances
   for low profit sales; investigate consumer problems with
   Company products.

EMPLOYER
CONTACT

Present employer is not aware of decision to consider change
and may not be contacted at this time.

RAY L. KIRCHER

1812 Darlington Street
Windsor, Ontario, L8L 5G4
Canada
Telephone: (416) 219-4622

OBJECTIVE   Sales

AREAS OF   Sales   Distributor Setup:
KNOWLEDGE   Personal Selling of Key   Contact, Control
AND   Accounts
EXPERIENCE   Distribution   Original Equipment Manu-
                                                      facturers
                     Sales Forecasting
                     Territory Layout   Sales to Retailers
                     Marketing   Sales to Wholesalers

PERSONAL   Birthdate: 4-6-47   Married, Two children
                     5'11"   170 Lbs.   Excellent Health

EDUCATION   Wayne University, Detroit
                       4 years College Credit
                         Major: Marketing   Minor: Advertising

EXPERIENCE
May, 1978   UNITED WIRE AND SUPPLY CORPORATION, Detroit, Michigan.
to Present   Producer of precision seamless drawn copper, copper alloy,
                     aluminum tube and low temperature brazing alloys.

                     Position: Sales Representative

                     Earnings: $29,000 (base and incentive)

                     Responsibilities:
                       -- Contact industrial manufacturers and fabricators in a 3-
                          state Midwest territory to obtain new business and estab-
                          lish a wider distribution of firm's products.
                       -- Service existing industrial and distributor accounts.
                       -- Establish new distributors; assist personnel and work
                          closely with them to promote business.

                     Achievements:
                       -- Increased sales volume in territory from a beginning of
                          $900,000 to a high of $4.2 million.
                       -- Personally ranked No. 1 in sales for the entire company
                          the last 3 years.
                       -- Sales Territory ranked in the top 2 producing areas in the
                          U.S. the last 4 years.
                       -- Successfully opened western Wisconsin and Minnesota; de-
                          veloped the area into a producing and profitable one.

May, 1975 May, 1978	GREAT WESTERN STEEL COMPANY, Chicago, Illinois. Steel warehouse; steel, sheetmetal, coil strip, processing.

Position: Industrial Sales Representative

Responsibilities and Achievements:
-- Sold carbon bars, shape, strip, sheets and coils to existing and potential O.E.M.'s, metal stamping steel fabricating and sheet metal accounts in the Chicago area.
-- Became familiar with firm's products, pricing, general operation and marketing through a period of sales desk training and participation in a management training program based in Milwaukee, Wisconsin.
-- In 3 years, developed non-productive Chicago territory into a productive, profitable area; increased sales by over 40%.

Apr., 1973 May, 1975	R. J. REYNOLDS TOBACCO CO., Winston Salem, North Carolina. Cigarette and food manufacturer.

Position: Sales Representative

Responsibilities and Achievements:
-- Responsible for gaining complete distribution of Company products in a specified sales territory: advertising, selling, promoting.
-- Called on wholesalers, chain stores, co-ops and direct retail accounts; given the responsibility of contacting wholesale and chain store accounts after just 3 months with the Company.

TRAVEL	Agreeable to any moderate amount of travel required.
LOCATION	Willing to relocate for the right opportunity.
EMPLOYER CONTACT	Present employer is not aware of decision to consider change and may not be contacted at this time.

ROSS E. HAYES

89 Cumberland Drive
Cambridge, MA 07698
Telephone: (617) 471-0905

OBJECTIVE   Sales Management

HIGHLIGHTS   As National Sales Director
OF CAREER   * Developed innovative approaches to selling department
                         stores.
                       * Initiated a Company weekly Idea Clearing House bulletin
                         which has achieved recognition as most stimulating in-
                         house merchandising tool.
                       * High level presentations created two major accounts:
                         Jones Store, Kansas City, and Kaufman's, Pittsburgh.

                   As National Accounts Manager
                       * Increased annual sales to J. C. Penney from $600,000 in
                         March, 1984 to $1.8 million by January, 1985.
                       * Developed unique marketing approach for J. C. Penney which
                         made use of both Batts and Penney names on merchandise for
                         the first time.
                       * Built total national account program by 30% in 1984 through
                         new merchandising and advertising.

                   As District Marketing Manager
                       * Expanded sales from $2.3 million (Jan., 1982) to $3.1 mil-
                         lion (December, 1983).
                       * Company's advertising exposure increased 50% in Chicago
                         market; became dominant supplier for two major accounts.
                       * Successfully handled key major accounts: Dayton's, Gimbel's,
                         Carson Pirie Scott, Milwaukee Boston, Prange.

                   As Territory Sales Representative
                       * Built New England sales from $769,000 (1977) to $2 million
                         (1981).
                       * Added key major accounts in Hartford, Rochester, Long Is-
                         land.
                       * Increased number of newspaper ads in New England over 25%.
                       * Successfully handled key major accounts: Forbes & Wallace,
                         G. Fox, The Outlet Company, Sibley's, Fortunoff.

                   As Salesman
                       * Consistent sales leader in the District.
                       * Increased sales 20% per year for 2 years; exceeded all
                         quotas.
                       * Rated No. 1 in District in building mail order sales.

148

AREAS OF KNOWLEDGE AND EXPERIENCE	Retail Merchandising and Marketing	Advertising Planning and Budgeting
	Sales Management	Major Account Presentations
	National Account Development and Handling	
	Personal Selling of Key Accounts	Pricing: Retail, Wholesale
		Selling Aids
		Retail Display
	Sales Promotion, Contests	Sales Meetings

PROFESSIONAL
MEMBERSHIP   International Home Furnishings Representatives Association

EDUCATION   Miami University, Oxford, Ohio
                   BA Degree - 1974
                     Major: Economics   Minor: Business Administration

EXPERIENCE
SUMMARY
Jan., 1984   BATTS, BOSTON.
to Present   Mattress manufacturer. Sales volume $200 million.

(Sept., 1984   Position: National Sales Director
to Present
                 Responsibilities:
                   -- Help develop and administer Batts merchandising and market-
                      ing programs nationally.
                   -- Participant, Batts Marketing and Sales Manager's Committees
                      which determine national marketing policies.
                   -- With Advertising Department, develop sales promotion and ad-
                      vertising plans, including sales training films and aids.
                   -- Make presentations to major accounts at highest corporate
                      levels.
                   -- Publish merchandising ideas bulletins.

(Jan., 1984   Position: National Accounts Manager
Sept., 1984)
                 Responsibilities:
                   -- Represent 35 licensed factories to major national accounts;
                      develop merchandising and marketing policies.
                   -- Administer retail and wholesale pricing.
                   -- Develop sales promotional ideas for major accounts; make
                      top-level presentations.

                 Reason for Change: Promoted to National Sales Director.

Oct., 1977 Dec., 1983	STEARNS & FOSTER, Cincinnati, Ohio. Manufacturers of mattresses and diversified products. Sales volume $75 million.
(Jan., 1982 Dec., 1983)	Position: District Marketing Manager

Responsibilities:
-- Create and implement marketing policies for Midwest District; administer pricing, retail and wholesale.
-- Sell major department stores and furniture stores in a 4-state Midwest area.
-- Develop advertising/promotional ideas for major department stores.
-- Improve merchandise displays; conduct floor salesmen education programs; maintain store stock control programs.
-- Coordinate major account newspaper advertising.
-- Counsel department store Advertising Departments on techniques of mattress advertising.

Reason for Change: Accepted an opportunity for management.

(Oct., 1977   Position: Territory Sales Representative
Jan., 1982)

Responsibilities:
-- Establish general merchandising policy for territory; determine retail and wholesale pricing structure.
-- Sell major department stores and furniture stores in a 6-state New England area; plan store advertising/promotional programs; conduct sales meetings; develop sales contests and promotion ideas.
-- Manage carload and truckload shipments.

Reason for Change: Promoted to District Marketing Manager.

Mar., 1975   SIMMONS CO., Columbus, Ohio. Manufacturers of mattresses and
Oct., 1977   diversified products. Sales volume $170 million.

Position: Salesman

Responsibilities: Sell and service established accounts; check stocks and maintain inventory levels; hold sales meetings. Acquire new accounts.

TRAVEL   Agreeable to unlimited travel.

LOCATE   Willing to relocate.

AVAILABILITY   30-60 days' notice required.

EMPLOYER   Present employer is not aware of decision to consider change
CONTACT   and may not be contacted at this time.

REFERENCES   References are available upon request.

SAMUEL T. CRAIG

1391 Skyway Blvd.
Chattanooga, TN 37126
Telephone: (615) 446-8207

OBJECTIVE   Sales/Marketing Management

SUMMARY   A successful sales/marketing executive -- thoroughly know-
               ledgeable and experienced in the techniques of selling ideas,
               products, and programs, augmented by a sound dealer and cus-
               tomer relations capability.

AREAS OF   Sales Management   Dealer Set-up, Control
SALES AND   General Management   Government Sales
MARKETING   Policy Determination
KNOWLEDGE
                                             Application Engineering
               Market Potential Evaluation   Research and Development
               Sales Forecasting
               Budgets   Purchasing

               Sales Supervision, Training   Cost Control
               Recruitment, Hiring
               Performance Appraisal   Pricing

               National Account Contact   Trade Shows
                                              Customer Relations

PERSONAL   Birthdate 7-7-44   Married, Two children
               5'10"   170 Lbs.   Excellent Health

EDUCATION   Temple University, Philadelphia, Pennsylvania 1966-1970
                  Major: Marketing   Minor: Advertising

EXPERIENCE
1978 to   MAJOR OFFICE EQUIPMENT MANUFACTURER, Boston, MA
Present
(Dec., 1981   Position: General Division Manager -- Southern Division
to Present)
               Responsibilities: Total sales and marketing effort with P&L
               responsibility; develop and implement national sales, service
               and administrative programs. Functions include: purchasing,
               sales training, product planning and testing, inventory analy-
               sis, advertising and sales promotional material, market surveys
               and analysis.

               Achievements:
               -- Increased net profit from 0% to 5.3% and unit sales from
                  $1,000 to $6,000; reduced inventory by $300,000.
               -- Built sales force from 20 to 50 men; directed successful
                  advertising and public relations programs.
               -- Opened new key accounts with total annual potential $1
                  million volume.

151

            -- Made substantial savings by reorganizing each territory
               for maximum coverage based on sales/expense budgets.
            -- Hired and trained 6 future Regional Managers, a National
               Accounts Manager, a National Training Manager.

(July, 1980   Position: Southern Marketing Manager - Atlanta
Dec., 1981)
                   Responsibilities: All marketing effort for a 9-state area with
                   300 sales, service and branch personnel.

                   Achievements:
                   -- Profits of the area accounted for 35% of the Division's
                      total on 25% of the Division's total volume.
                   -- Increased total sales 60% over previous year.
                   -- Developed a national accounts program which resulted in a
                      40% increase in key national account sales and coverage.
                   -- Evaluated the market potential for new products; recommen-
                      dation accepted and a Company was acquired.

(July, 1978   Position: Zone Manager - New Jersey
July, 1980)
                   Responsibilities: Sales, service and administration for terri-
                   tory consisting of New Jersey and Upstate New York.

                   Achievements:
                   -- Developed sales programs utilizing advanced telephone tech-
                      niques; Zone result was retention of 80% of the business;
                      plan adopted nationally.
                   -- Zone became first nationally in Company sales.
                   -- Increased Zone volume from $75,000 to $165,000 monthly.

(Feb., 1978   Position: Regional Manager - New York City
July, 1978)   Supervise 35 salesmen in Lower Manhattan; top Region in
                      overall sales performance 4 out of 6 months nationally; per-
                      sonally opened 10 new major accounts.

1974   ART METAL, INC., Jamestown, New York
1978   Office equipment manufacturer.

                   Position: Midwest Regional Sales Manager, after promotions.
                      Supervise 2 direct Branches (Chicago, Detroit) plus coordi-
                      nating 12-state dealer network sales programs.

1971   REMINGTON RAND, Philadelphia
1974
                   Position; Sales Representative

TRAVEL   Agreeable to unlimited travel.

LOCATE   Willing to relocate.

AVAILABILITY   30 days' notice required.

EMPLOYER   Present employer is not aware of decision to consider change
CONTACT   and may not be contacted at this time.

MICHELE HAINES

2916 Western Boulevard
Vancouver, B.C. V6B 1X2
Canada
Telephone: (604) 432-4718

OBJECTIVE	Sales Supervision-Clothing	

AREAS OF	General Retail Chain	Full Profit Responsibility
KNOWLEDGE	Management	
AND	Sales Management	New Store Openings
EXPERIENCE	Operating Procedures	
	Policy Determination	Sales Promotions, Contests
	Merchandising	Displays
		Advertising
	Recruiting, Hiring	
	Sales Training	Customer Relations
	Security	

PERSONAL	Birthdate: 1-24-60	Single
	5'8" 125 Lbs.	Excellent Health

EDUCATION	University of Washington, Seattle
	B.S. Degree
	Major: Fashion Merchandising Minor: Business

EXPERIENCE June, 1983 to Present	UPS 'N DOWNS, INC., Vancouver, B.C. Retail chain (women's junior sportswear); sales volume $30 million; 89 stores.
(Mar., 1984 to Present)	Position: District Manager - Vancouver area Responsibilities: -- As District Manager, responsibilities include overall management and supervision of 5 stores doing an annual volume of $3 million. -- Overall responsibility for sales, merchandising and inventory control. -- Working through store managers, supervise a total staff of 60 employees; handle employee and customer relations, incentives, salary administration. -- Recruit and train personnel.

153

Achievements:
-- Assigned responsibility of highest volume territory in the entire chain.
-- Increased sales volume in first 3 stores 20%, 24%, and 58% over previous year's figures.
-- Increased ratings of individual stores based on sales volume from 5 to 3, 7 to 4 and 47 to 28 respectively.
-- Decreased shrinkage in respective stores from 4.6% to 3.4%, 9.7% to 3.9% and 11.5% to 2.6% in 8 months.
-- Promoted from Store Manager to District Manager in 10 months.

(June, 1983
Feb., 1984)

Position: Store Manager - Evergreen Lake Plaza (6/83-8/83)
                           Burnfield Shopping Center (8/83-2/84)

Responsibilities:
-- Direct and manage overall store operations for stores doing $750,000 annual volume, 15 employees; sales, merchandising, customer service, staff supervision and motivation, employee scheduling and inventory control.

Achievements:
-- Increased Burnfield store rating from 15th to 7th in 5 months (63 stores in the chain).
-- Decreased shrinkage from 6.8% to 4.7% during a 5 month period at Burnfield.

Sept., 1982
May, 1983

BALKIN AND TINOFF, Minneapolis, Minnesota.
Retail men's and women's clothing chain. Sales volume $40 million; 150 stores.

Position: Store Manager

Responsibilities:
-- Store management responsibilities basically the same as with Ups 'n Downs stores at Evergreen Lake and Burnfield.
-- Full profit responsibility for store having $350,000 gross sales, handling fashion irregulars and special purchases.
-- Full responsibility for pricing increases over established retail, and markdowns.
-- Assumed the responsibility of creating promotion and advertising messages for radio advertising.

Achievements:
-- Opened new store after one month's training; maintained a shrinkage of .9%.
-- Ranked number one in sales volume in the 4 store Division.

EMPLOYER
CONTACT

Present employer is not aware of decision to consider a change and may not be contacted at this time.

154

THEODORE ASHLEY

2198 Eastern Parkway
Richmond, VA 08921
Telephone: (804) 978-0026

OBJECTIVE

President/General Manager/Vice President

Senior Financial Management

HIGHLIGHTS
OF CAREER
BACKGROUND

As President: Manufacturing Company

.. Turned loss operation into profitable operation in first
year as President.
.. Increased sales volume from $750,000 to over $2 million
per year (1980-1985).
.. Moved plant and expanded production facilities fourfold.
.. Obtained Quality Assurance approval (AEC requirements) for
nuclear plant construction.

As Controller

.. Assisted in turning Energy Products Group from $1 million
annual loss to $1.5 million annual profit in less than 18
months.
.. Designed and installed automated standard job cost system
which enabled Production management to isolate and identify
material and efficiency variances rapidly and reliably.
.. Designed and implemented corporate system of pricing inter-
plant and intercompany sales.

As Corporate Controller

.. Helped Company to achieve a sales growth in excess of 15%
per year.
.. Implemented cost reduction programs which resulted in turning operations from loss to profit position in one year.
.. Designed and installed computerized management information
system.

AREAS OF
KNOWLEDGE
AND
EXPERIENCE

Full Profit Responsibility	Cash Flow
General Management	Budgets and Forecasts
	Cost Control
Organization Structure	
Policy Determination	Manufacturing/Production
Operation Procedures	Marketing
Acquisitions and Dispositions	Distributors
Pricing and Margins	
Financing	Customer Relations

EDUCATION   DePaul University, Chicago, Illinois
                         MBA Degree - 1978
                      Case Western Reserve University, Cleveland, Ohio
                         BBA Degree - 1966

                      Special Training: Various seminars on Production, Maintenance,
                      Marketing and Financial Matters

PROFESSIONAL
MEMBERSHIP   American Institute of CPAs.

CERTIFICATION   Certified Public Accountant: State of Illinois - 1972

EXPERIENCE
SUMMARY
1980 to   EXETER MANUFACTURING COMPANY, Richmond, VA.
Present   Fabricator of miscellaneous metals for use in construction of
                     water treatment plants, power plants and steel mills. Annual
                     sales $2 million plus; 50 employees.

                     Position: President

                     Earnings: Base salary, profit sharing, car and expenses.

                     Responsibilities:
                     -- Set corporate policies for marketing and contract bidding.
                     -- Completely responsible for corporate profit.
                     -- Manage Marketing, Production, Engineering and Finance func-
                        tions through function managers.
                     -- Personally contact large engineering and construction cus-
                        tomers.
                     -- Negotiate pricing and close all contracts amounting to
                        $50,000 or more.

1978   BAYLOR FORGE, INC., Palatine, IL.
1980   Manufacturer of forgings, fittings, and piping products. Annual
                     sales volume $110 million; 2500 employees.

                     Position: Controller - Energy Products Group
                               Annual sales $60 million; 1500 employees.

                     Responsibilities:
                     -- Line responsibility for all Accounting, Financial Planning
                        and Control functions of largest Group within corporation.
                     -- Direct the activities of a staff of 35 employees.

1974   CLOSURES CORPORATION OF AMERICA, Chicago.
1978   Manufacturer of flexible packaging products for use in the food
                     industry. Annual sales $17 million; 500 employees.

                     Position: Corporate Controller (Chief Financial Officer), re-
                               porting to the President.

156

Responsibilities:
-- Line responsibility for Accounting, Data Processing, Taxes, and Corporate and Financial Planning functions.
-- Serve as member of Executive Committee.
-- Handle financing and banking relationships.
-- Establish and chair Pricing Committee.

Reason for Change: Accepted an equivalent position with greater earnings in larger company.

PRIOR
EXPERIENCE

MARK CONTROLS, INC., Evanston, Illinois. 1971-1974
Manufacturer of water well drilling equipment and industrial valves. Annual sales $20 million; 600 employees.

Position: Manager of Internal Accounting. Supervised Cost, Budgeting, Auditing and Timekeeping Departments.

CRAFTINT MANUFACTURING COMPANY, INC., Chicago. 1968-1971
Manufacturer of art supplies. Annual sales $3.5 million.

Position: Assistant Controller. Responsible for Cost Accounting and Auditing functions.

ARTHUR ANDERSEN & COMPANY, Chicago. 1966-1968

Position; Staff Auditor - Manufacturing Group.

ACADEMIC
EXPERIENCE

Roosevelt University: Lecturer in CDP Review Course
University of Illinois: Lecturer in Accounting
John Marshall Law School: Lecturer in Accounting
Loyola University: Lecturer in Accounting and Systems.

TRAVEL

Agreeable to travel -- up to 25%.

LOCATION

Prefer to remain in the Eastern Seaboard area.

AVAILABILITY

30 days' notice required.

REFERENCES

Available upon request.

SUSAN SMITH GOFF

7712 South Indiana Avenue
Chicago, IL 60619
Telephone: (312) 725-8617 (Home)
          (312) 385-0672 (Office)

OBJECTIVE	Management/Supervision: Social Work

AREAS OF
KNOWLEDGE
AND
EXPERIENCE

Social Welfare/Health	Nursing Center Administration
Program Planning/Analysis	Policy Formation
Liaison/Advisory	
	Nursing Care
Personal Counseling	Medical, Professional Liaison
Casework	Paraprofessional Supervision
Referral Service	
Investigations, Claims	Staff Training
Interviewing	Union Relations

PERSONAL

Birthdate 6-11-39	Married, Three Children
5'6" 150 Lbs.	Excellent Health

EDUCATION

Indiana University Graduate School of Social Work
  M.A. Degree in Social Work - 1961
Butler University, Indianapolis, Indiana
  B.A. Degree - 1959
    Major: Sociology   Minor: Psychology

Special Training: Social Casework and Supervision; Human De-
velopment; Preschool Children; Role of the Parent; Aging
Process of Man; Role of the Staff and Relationships to the
Elderly Person.

EXPERIENCE
Mar., 1981
to Present
(Mar., 1982
to Present)

CAROL ANN NURSING HOMES, INC., Skokie, Illinois

Position: Administrator -- Hyde Park Nursing Center
          Extended care facility; 152 bed capacity.

Responsibilities as Administrator:
  -- Overall responsibility for the administration of the Cen-
     ter; final responsibility for the care of the patients/
     residents.
  -- Direct the Managers of the 5 Departments: nursing, dietary,
     building and maintenance, activities, business.
  -- Control the business aspects of the total operation: bud-
     gets, finances, bookkeeping, billing, accounts receivable,
     payroll, purchasing, maintenance.
  -- Handle staffing, employment, training, discipline, union
     relations.

-- Maintain liaison with governmental/regulatory agencies for compliance with regulations: inspections; statistical data.
-- Coordinate activities of entire staff and consultants; close liaison with medical/professional staff and paraprofessionals.
-- Build and maintain public relations/community relations.
-- Supervise 26 professionals and 46 paraprofessionals.

(Mar., 1981
Mar., 1982)

Position: Social Work Consultant

Responsibilities:
-- Work with the Administrators and staffs of 4 nursing homes, 2 skilled and 2 intermediate; plan and implement in-service training programs to strengthen staff members' knowledge of psycho-social problems of the aged and disabled.
-- Assist the Administrators and Company management with employee problems.

1968
1979
(1977-1979)

YWCA OF METROPOLITAN CHICAGO

Positions: Director - South Parkway YWCA Center
             Coordinator - Child Development Center

Combined Responsibilities:
-- Design and offer to the community a total program to meet the needs of the total family group: preschool age through senior citizens.
-- Plan the program to include education, recreation, health, nutrition, job skills, leadership development.
-- Supervise and coordinate YWCA staff of 15 and a Child Development staff of 24.
-- Train and motivate the entire staff to become an effective team.
-- Raise the level of community involvement with the program.
-- Create a Center Volunteer Group of professionals and nonprofessionals to set policies, raise funds, sustain an image and work with the YWCA Board.

(1975-1977)

Position: Coordinator - YWCA Headstart Program

Responsibilities:
-- After the original summer program in 2 sites, design and develop a full year round program at South Parkway YWCA for 60 children.
-- Maintain the program in accordance with licensing agencies and follow federal and state guidelines; prepare and submit annual proposal to OEO.
-- Train the staff; order supplies; maintain inventory; prepare statistics and reports; liaison with OEO and YWCA staff.

                             -- Provide an educational and recreational program for chil-
                                dren; create a health program; build parent interest;
                                locate and utilize community resources.

(1969-1974)   Position: Director - YWCA Personal Service Dept.

                   Responsibilities:
                    -- Provide a service of short-term counseling to any young
                       person, male and female, in areas of jobs, education,
                       housing, personal problem solving.
                    -- Coordinate orientation and in-service training to staff.
                    -- Supervise 3 professionals and a clerical staff.
                    -- Formulate policy; prepare budgets; build and sustain a
                       volunteer committee; become involved in fund raising and
                       working with community groups.

(1968-1969)   Position: Caseworker - YWCA Personal Service Dept.

                   Responsibilities:
                    -- Handle normal casework duties, as outlined above.

1962   YOUTH GUIDANCE, Chicago.
1967
                   Positions: Assistant Director (1964-1967)
                              Caseworker (1962-1967)

                   Responsibilities:
                    -- Counseled emotionally disturbed young girls and unwed
                       mothers; arranged foster home and adoption placements.

1961   LAKE COUNTY DEPT. OF WELFARE, Gary, Indiana
1962
                   Position: Caseworker -- ADC, Old Age, Blind Assistance, Gene-
                             ral Assistance.

LOCATION   Prefer to remain in the Chicago area.

AVAILABILITY   30 days' notice required.

EMPLOYER   Present employer is not aware of decision to consider change
CONTACT   and may not be contacted at this time.

LEWIS WARFIELD

6704 W. Bixley Street
Toronto, Ontario M4R 1B9
Canada
Telephone: (416) 324-6038

OBJECTIVE   General Traffic Manager

                   -- Industrial Organization

AREAS OF   Traffic Administration   Trucking and Equipment
KNOWLEDGE   Shipping and Receiving
                   Transportation   Dispatching

                   Distribution   Materials Handling & Equip-
                                                        ment
                   Warehousing
                   Inventory Control   Packaging

                   Plant Site Selection   Equipment Utilization Stan-
                                                        dards
                   Freight Classification   Employee Productivity Stan-
                       Changes   dards
                   Rate Adjustments
                                                    Budgeting
                   Loss and Damage Claims
                                                    Union Negotiation
                   Travel Arrangements
                                                    Procedure Writing & Imple-
                                                        mentation
                   Fleet Car Administration

                   Garage Administration

EXPERIENCE
1975   CONSOLIDATED PACKAGING CORPORATION, Toronto, Ontario.
to Present   Manufacturer of paper products; approximate sales volume, $70
                   million; 3,000 employees.

                   Positions: Corporate Director of Transportation
                              Director of Transportation

                   Responsibilities: Direct charge of all transportation activities
                   at 18 manufacturing facilities: all shipping, receiving, and
                   warehousing activities; corporate transportation policies, pro-
                   curement of trucking and materials handling equipment and sup-
                   plies; union negotiations.

161

Achievements:
-- Reorganized corporate private trucking activities to
   function as a commercial carrier and as a separate profit
   center. 1985 reported earnings were $181,217.

-- Negotiated a rail rate adjustment, saving $38,000 per
   year.

-- Accomplished a 10% reduction in drivers and a 21% reduction in trailer equipment by establishing successful driver
   productivity and trailer utilization standards.

-- Effected annual savings of over $35,000 by negotiating
   (1980) 23 freight rate adjustments.

-- Successfully standardized trucking and materials handling
   equipment for all plants.

-- Established effective controls over plant transportation
   expenses by designing and installing reporting and audit
   procedures.

1960
1975

FEDERAL PAPERBOARD, INC., Toronto, Ontario; manufacturer of
paper products; annual sales approximately $110 million; 4,000
employees.

Position: General Traffic Manager, following promotion from
          Traffic Manager

Responsibilities; As General Traffic Manager and member of
management staff, was responsible for:
-- operation and profitability of 4 manufacturing plants
-- all transportation, warehousing, inventory control, and
   materials handling; including equipment acquisitions
-- general management of a subsidiary for-hire truck carrier
-- union negotiations

Achievements:
-- Introduced use of paper pallets, with annual savings of over
   $12,000.

-- Saved over $75,000 per year by redesigning warehouse facili-
   ties and improving inventory control practices.

-- Initiated a small, private trucking operation which gene-
   rated savings averaging $35,000 per year for five years.

-- Secured two favorable Classification rulings which reduced
   freight expense by 15%.

-- Improved marketing in areas beyond 500 miles of plant location, by establishing rail commodity rates.

1955
1960

LESTRADE MANUFACTURING COMPANY, Toronto, Ontario

<u>Positions</u>: Assistant to Traffic Manager, following promotions
from: Rate Supervisor
Claim Supervisor
Warehousing Supervisor

AVAILABILITY   Immediate.

EMPLOYER   Resignation accomplished; previous employer may be contacted
CONTACT   at once.

TRAVEL   Agreeable to any amount normally consistent with this position.

LOCATION   Readily willing to relocate.

MEMBERSHIPS   Canadian Industrial Traffic League -- Committee Member
International Materials Handling Society -- Member
Canadian Truck Council -- Committee Member

PART
II

Writing and Producing Your Résumé

Writing Your Résumé Draft

Managers and executives tend to want to do it now—whatever it is. A great deal of organizational and professional activity involves meeting a deadline. Business and industrial activities, in particular, operate against deadlines. So what do executives often do when they decide to write a résumé? They start right in. They shouldn't. A less-than-ideal résumé will usually be the result.

Before you begin to write your résumé, you must study, ponder, and decide what should be included, based on your experiences, achievements, and an understanding of what a potential employer wants to read.

YOUR STRENGTHS

Your strengths must shine forth. Do not list these; show them by presenting the results of past performance. This excellent résumé material may well be hidden deep down inside you.

This is where thought comes in. Reflect on just what your best areas are. Can you get things done through people? (Never say that you enjoy "working with people"; good managers know that working with people is exasperating, difficult, necessary, frustrating, and not all that enjoyable.) Can you administer efficiently and decisively? Do you have vision? In sales, for example, is it your personality that makes you click? What do you do best? What do you enjoy most?

YOUR WEAKNESSES

Next, bring your weaknesses to the surface. You normally don't think too much about them. It's painful. Whether you talk this over with someone or dig them out yourself doesn't matter. (The people who know you best are your ex-bosses, but they probably won't tell you.) What you want are the facts. Here are a few thought-starters: Do you procrastinate? Work well below your full capacity? Fail to discipline your subordinates correctly? Cover up your errors? Fail to give credit when it is due? Do you try to look important by doing "busy work"?

Think about your weaknesses. Determine to overcome these negatives. There is no need to discuss this soul-searching with anyone; just learn from it. Nobody is right 100 percent of the time. If 90 percent of your decisions prove to be right, you're a genius. (Never list any weaknesses in your résumé. Remember, your résumé is your sales tool, so it must be positive.)

DRAFT DESIGN AND PREPARATION

Your résumé must make a great first impression—not good or average, but great. This has no reference to content but to the reaction of a reader as he or she takes a quick look at your résumé for the first time. Here are some of the immediate, unspoken questions he or she will ask:

1. Is it neat and well put together?
2. Is it easy to read? Is there enough white space around the copy?
3. Is it well typed?
4. Is the paper of good quality?

This initial look takes about five or six seconds; you either get a positive start with the reader, or you don't. Keep this in mind as you plan your layout, arrange for the typing, and order the printing.

Executive and managerial experience shows that the most qualified applicant often does not get the job. Why not? Shouldn't merit prevail? Sure it should, but many other factors have influence, including the quality of your résumé, how you handle an interview, and sometimes whom you know. As chapter 2 points out, your executive résumé may be your first opportunity to display your communication skills. Make the most of it!

As any professional ad writer will tell you, good design involves layout, use of the right type, and—an essential—white space. Since the first impression is vital, the design and layout of your résumé is crucial. Here are the rules:

1. Use 8½-by-11-inch paper.
2. Leave plenty of white space; don't crowd the page.
3. Typed material should be balanced and orderly.
4. Use short paragraphs.
5. Use concise, clear sentences.
6. Left-hand margins must be even.
7. Use emphasis devices (capitals, underlining, dots, asterisks) but not in excess.
8. Grammar and spelling must be perfect.

Don't expect to do a final draft until you've written several preliminary drafts. No one can, not even a pro. A fine executive résumé layout is the result of successive efforts. When you think you've got it right, ask yourself, "Is this my best?"; "Is it result-oriented?"; "Is it written for the employer and not for me?"; "Am I communicating well about myself?"

PREPARING YOUR PERSONAL SALES TOOL

As you write your first draft, break with custom. You're selling *yourself* now, so give your prose some creative life. Let it be you, not a collection of dull, repetitive sentences. You have contributed elsewhere; you are worth considering for that new position. Say so, with honesty, without ego, but with enthusiasm in the words and sentences. Present that "you" in the most favorable light. Caution: Avoid slick language that reads too smoothly. Do you really talk that way?

JUST BEFORE YOU WRITE

If you haven't come to a final conclusion about the type of résumé you want, review chapter 5. Which style will best serve you? Your layout will be based on the style you select or modify. Have all your material sorted into the basic areas or parts, so that you can quickly go from your name and address on down. Run through the collected items in each part and choose what you want to use.

NOW WRITE

Remember these key elements: (1) name and address; (2) objective; (3) knowledge and experience highlights (which you may or may not include, depending on the style of

your résumé); (4) work experience; (5) education; (6) professional status, if applicable.

Other areas of information that will probably appear on many professional/managerial/executive résumés include availability, present employer contact, relocation, and personal.

Achievements are paramount, as you know. Have you condensed and rephrased them until you are satisfied? Here is where you use "Action-Power" words such as those listed below. You can doubtless come up with additional action verbs, adverbs, and nouns. If a word is truly accurate, use it. Employers and interviewers do not appreciate self-glorification, however, so use Action-Power words with great care:

Accomplished
Built
Competent
Controlled
Designed
Directed
Eliminated
Expanded
Experienced
Increased
Introduced
Managed
Productive
Profitably
Professional
Qualified
Reduced
Thoroughly

NOW TYPE

Type your first draft or have it typed. How many uncrowded typed pages are there? One, two, or three pages are normal. Two or three easy-to-read pages are better than one or two crowded sheets. Even one page is fine, if you can include all your pertinent data and still have plenty of white space. This can be very difficult to accomplish, of course, if you have ten, twenty, or more years of work experience. Never use more than three pages. Refine this draft. Before you retype your résumé, check for these error possibilities:

Errors in spelling
Errors in grammar
Sentences too long
Paragraphs too long
Entire résumé too long
Results not stressed enough
Proofreading not done
Anything else you can think of

A second or even a third draft should give you an effective sales tool.

Now you rush to the typing service, right? Not quite. You rush to your confidant, someone who will tell you what's wrong with your pride-and-joy résumé. In this discussion, your goal is not compliments, it's improvements. This outside look can do wonders in opening your eyes as well as in catching errors. Your reader-friend should be a person who has done hiring, who has seen lots of résumés, good and bad—someone who will be truthful about how to make your résumé a more effective sales tool.

HOW MANY VERSIONS?

The number of different résumés you prepare depends on your needs. One universal, all-purpose résumé seems to work for many executive and professional positions, but not for all. If you are searching in several fields, or for unrelated position titles, write and print second and third versions. Your employer versions may include one without an objective (which is handled by your cover letter), and one or more with objectives. Employer versions need less detail on such items as vital statistics, and some items, such as Reason for Change and References, should be omitted.

You may want a special version for executive search consultants, who insist on your birthdate, marital status, and other personal items. They also want to know all about your present and past work history.

Multiple versions cost more money, sometimes a lot more. Still, this extra investment can bring more satisfactory returns.

Résumé Writing Services

What if you can't write your executive résumé yourself? Perhaps you can't quite get to it. Well, don't procrastinate or you may pay dearly. Perhaps the draft of your résumé doesn't come easily to you, even after you've put hours into collecting your background material. You want to do it yourself, but writing isn't one of your best skills.

If you decide you can't compose a first-class executive résumé, then find someone who can. Do you repair your car by yourself, or do you hire a mechanic to do it for you? Do you paint your house or decorate your apartment the way a pro does? No one can do everything well. So, if you need résumé composition and/or job-search counsel, get it. Get the best help you can. Go to a professional résumé writer who is competent, experienced, and willing to work for you as an individual. For your part, be willing to pay for this help and guidance. The cost of a good executive résumé should be measured against the tens of thousands of dollars you expect to earn in the next few years. Perhaps even more to the point, an effective résumé can be measured against the satisfaction you hope to achieve in doing work you enjoy for an organization you have selected.

A capable, sincere résumé preparation practitioner offers you these things:

- An outside viewpoint that may be helpful.
- The skill and experience you do not possess.
- Time saving.
- An understanding of the market.
- A supportive attitude.
- A broad knowledge of what *not* to say and do.
- A second opinion on a draft you've already made.

Finding the right person for the job isn't always easy, but it's wise to be selective. Get a recommendation from a business or personal friend who has used such a service (if you can afford to let him or her know about your job search). Visit two or three services and look them over. Do get costs for comparison, but more important, try to select a counselor who is right for you.

If you have no leads at all, start with the Yellow Pages for the city where you expect to have the work done. Look under "Résumé Service." In Chicago, for example, you'll find as many as thirty-five to forty such listings. In Seattle, you will find thirty-seven, in Detroit, twenty, in Denver, forty-one, in Atlanta, thirty-six, in Omaha, eleven, and in Charlotte, NC, seventeen. Your public library often has out-of-town telephone books.

You should generally exclude the typing services, printers, and stationery stores that list themselves as résumé services. You need a professional, not an individual who has typed one hundred résumés but composed none. Now you should consider whether or not the national or local chains are right for you. Some have up to ten offices in a major city. Is there a capable counselor in each office, or a salesperson? You'll know when you visit. Study the ads in the Yellow Pages. The largest ad may or may not represent the best service. Would you select a firm because it offers you "instant service" or "one-day service"? How about the "free résumé analysis or cover-letter brochure"? On the positive side, if an appointment is required to discuss the work, that may be a good sign. Sometimes the best service might have a counselor available when you walk in for the first time, right off the street.

What does a top-notch service charge? It depends on what they do for you. Are you buying résumé composition only and planning to handle the printing separately? If so, buy one camera-ready copy, which must include a final draft review that you make. Do you want the service to handle printing for you? If so, what quality paper (in your case, a white or lightly colored 25 percent rag bond) and how many copies? Do you want job-search guidance? Fees for individual consultation and résumé preparation may vary from $100 to $400 or more, depending on who does it, and, to some extent, the size of the city where the service is located.

What if you have no résumé service in your town or can't get to a metropolitan area? Check with your local college or university placement department for possibilities or recommendations of services. If such a person offers to do your résumé for you, you might want to ask what his or her experience has been in preparing résumés for managers or executives or professionals with a work background similar to yours. Failing that, you might consider the large city firms that handle résumé preparation by mail. Write to several to find out what is offered and for how much. Then make your selection or decide to write it yourself after all. It might be a wise decision.

9

Producing Your Résumé

What is the next step, now that you have prepared a top-quality executive résumé? Continue the top-quality theme as you arrange for the typing and printing.

TYPING

Your ability to type well isn't always in direct correlation with your professional, management, or executive ability. So even if you have personally typed your several drafts, spend the few dollars and let a typing service do the final draft for the printer, unless you are truly an expert typist. You want a service that will follow your layout instructions, use reasonably new equipment, and do the work promptly. While not essential, if the equipment can produce italics or boldface, these can be useful for emphasizing words or phrases in your résumé. The typewriter must produce a sharp, clear, black image so that your printer will get good copies from the offset press.

If the typing service has a typewriter with a memory device, so much the better. Your inevitable corrections in layout can be done faster and cheaper, without the typist redoing the entire page.

Should you consider having a printer set type for your draft? No—this will probably cause an unfavorable reaction in your reader, whoever he or she is. Custom has it that résumés are typed. Period. Furthermore, modern typing can provide different type styles, if you feel you need them. However, in certain fields or lines of work, it is common to submit typeset résumés. For example, graphic artists, typesetters, and publishing professionals may well follow this route.

What type style should you select? Should you use pica or elite? It doesn't really matter, as long as the type is easy to read and isn't too unusual. Remember, you are making

your "first impression." You want your résumé reader to give quick-glance approval to layout and typing and *then* start reading, or at least skimming, the contents. Type style doesn't get you an interview; content does. Standard 8½-by-11-inch paper is expected and should be used.

Check out several services; you want the best, not the cheapest. Ask to see samples of their typing, especially résumés. Decide which service offers the best quality.

Cost for typing can be by the page, by the hour, or by the job. Rates vary, depending on service location, service size, competition, and size of community. You should personally proofread the final typed version prior to printing.

PRINTING

Fine-quality offset printing is the best way to reproduce your résumé, assuming that your printer takes pride in the finished product and runs good clean copies, and that you have chosen the correct paper. Every community has one or more "fast printers." These services are capable of doing an excellent job; so are the small commercial printers. Check samples: Select a good one.

Paper stock should be twenty-four-pound white bond, with a 25 percent rag content, not a sulfite bond, or a printer's "just-as-good bond." Fifty percent or 100 percent rag paper is wasteful and unnecessary. Twenty-pound stock and sulfite bond is what most people get from a fast printer, unless they specify and pay for the better paper. If you prefer a colored stock, and many executives do, go right ahead. But specify off-white, ivory, or very pale beige. Avoid heavy shades.

Sometimes you will know that only a handful of résumés will be needed, perhaps six or twelve. Some photocopy services now use state-of-the-art machines and

172

provide excellent quality copies on a wide variety of paper stocks and colors. Cost is minimal at twenty to twenty-five cents per sheet. Inspect a sample before you order. Remember, quality is of paramount importance.

Photocopies from your local library will not do. They are great for copies of most everything but not for executive résumés. Of course, in a real emergency, such a copy might have to serve.

How many copies will you need? Maybe more than you think, so be generous.

Before you visit a printer and place your order, decide on the number of copies you will need for employer mailings, for ad answering, for executive search consultant mailings, for your contacts, for your own use, and for a reserve. It's cheaper to run more now than to be short and have to rerun. Also, when you begin to run out of résumés, you might tend to conserve the few you have left. That's a mistake. Your emphasis is on getting job interviews by *using* résumés, not on saving résumés.

An individually typed résumé can be used in isolated cases, to give you a customized product for a specific situation where your normal, printed versions do not fit. The need seldom arises, especially if you print one set of résumés without an objective and use your cover letter to bring out your job or career objective.

If your résumé has two or three pages, gather each set and staple it in the upper left-hand corner; this is a small security measure to keep the set together when it might be one of dozens or scores on somebody's desk.

It might occur to you to consider attaching a photograph to your résumé. There are a number of reasons why you should *not* do so, the primary one being that a potential employer is not interested in what you look like but in what he or she believes you might do for the organization or for him or her personally.

PART III

Getting
the
Job

Cover Letters

A well-written cover letter is an essential part of your job-search activity; it accompanies your want-ad responses, employer résumés, and résumés to executive search consultants. Cover letters, usually written as informal notes, go along with your résumés to business friends and personal contacts. Selling yourself by mail uncovers leads. Leads result in interviews. Interviews bring job offers. An outstanding cover letter will generally intrigue a reader enough for him or her to decide at least to skim the résumé enclosed. A poor letter creates a neutral reaction at best. At worst, it results in a discarded résumé.

LETTER MECHANICS

Letters must be clearly typed, following these guidelines: Use individual letters for those employers who will not be served by a general mass-mailing letter, for want ads, and for your contacts. Letters typed automatically are fine for mass mailings to potential employers and executive recruiters. Such letters should be personalized on the inside name and address with the same automatic typewriter or computer printer. Fill-ins on another machine rarely match perfectly, so should not be used.

Never print a letter. Hand sign all of your letters, no matter how many you have to do. Watch your spelling and grammar. Proofread.

HOW TO ADDRESS LETTERS

When writing to an executive search consultant, address your letter to a principal in the firm. (See the Appendix for a recommended source of these names.) When writing to an employer, address your letter to an individual who can hire you. A little research will turn up these names. If you are doing a large mass mailing to businesses, and this research isn't feasible, address your envelope to a title, such as Vice-President, Sales, or whatever is fitting, and use this title for the inside address. The letter salutation is a different matter. Your safest bet is to use "Dear Sir/Madam."

In a mailing to a professional, business, or industry association, or to a not-for-profit foundation, address letters to "Executive Director" unless you are shooting for that position. In that case, you need to find out the name of the president or chairman of the board and address your letter to that individual at his or her place of work, not at the association or foundation headquarters.

Mail addressed to a corporate president by name will reach that person's office but might not get through to the individual. Secretarial screening will probably route your letter to another key person who may be interested. Your letter might get through, however, depending on the practice of the individual in the top position. Letters addressed to "President" by title only most likely will *not* get through. That's why extra digging to get accurate names is worth the effort.

WHAT TO SAY IN A LETTER

A good job-search cover letter:

1. Is an aggressive letter (not egotistic, not boastful, but demonstrating a positive attitude).
2. Opens with a real attention getter, to capture the reader's interest.
3. Justifies your statements through examples.
4. Requests an interview.
5. Is written through the eyes of the employer. (Try to determine his or her goals, and write accordingly.)

6. Is short; one-page maximum.

7. Does not repeat what is in the résumé.

Let all your correspondence reflect your positive, even enthusiastic attitude. Show an individual how well you can communicate.

MAILING IDEAS

Use carefully chosen commemorative stamps for first-class mail. Perhaps an ordinary jobseeker thinks a stamp is a stamp. Not so. You are special, so watch even the little things.

Deposit letters in the post office or mailbox on Monday so that their arrival is timed for the middle of the week, not Friday or Monday. On Friday the recipient is likely to put your letter aside until later, perhaps just because he or she is thinking about weekend plans. On Monday, there is always a bigger volume of mail to go through, superiors give new directives, and subordinates bring up for discussion their new problems. Your letter doesn't stand much chance of being given the quiet attention you seek. For longer distances, time your mailing accordingly.

Don't rush to answer want ads. Almost nobody fills a top-level position in a couple of weeks, so let the flood of responses come in first. Time your letter to arrive about a week after the first ones do.

ALICE O'LEARY
2217 Clearwater Road, Apt. 206
Orlando, FL 32713
Phone: (813) 776-4216

Date

Ms. Margaret Sampson
Florida's Cypress Gardens
Highway 51
Winter Park, FL 32341

Dear Ms. Sampson:

Persuading people to increase an organization's sales or profits is my profession.
My success has been in Sales, Public Relations, and Customer Relations.

I am now changing positions, and I'd like very much to come in and chat with you
or another executive for about 20 minutes, because I believe that I can make a
strong contribution in my areas of knowledge and experience.

My objective is the opportunity for job satisfaction in utilizing my abilities and
experience to the fullest extent. The challenge of continued growth is important to
me.

Here is where I can be most effective:

Public Relations
Customer Relations
Sales and Sales Promotion
Persuasion and Liaison

My résumé is enclosed. I'll be happy to talk with you at your request.

May I hear from you?

Cordially,

Alice O'Leary

Enc.

JACK P. NEWTON
29 Palos Heights Avenue
Los Angeles, CA 90087
Phone: (213) 842-2371

Date

Mr. Alex W. Beeson, Chief Executive Officer
Consolidated Companies, Inc.
San Mendez Highway
Los Angeles, CA 90082

Dear Mr. Beeson:

For almost ten years I have been engaged in the task of taking over the
management of companies or divisions that were in trouble or heading that way
and turning these businesses into profitmakers. This has been a strenuous and
rewarding way to make a living. Since it generally resulted in the sale or merger
of the company involved, it has caused me to uproot my family more times than I
like.

At this particular moment, the wholly owned subsidiary corporation that I am
managing is in the final stages of being sold, and I doubt that there now exists in
the parent company a spot that will exercise my entrepreneurial skills.

I am, therefore, interested in finding a company—probably (but not necessarily)
one that has had inadequate growth or profitability and that needs new
management. Preferably this should be a company in which I could take a
significant equity position and help develop into a really profitable growing
enterprise.

While I am now earning a substantial yearly salary in addition to a bonus
arrangement and options, my interest in a high base is not great, and I would
much rather have superior performance compensated through some form of
capital gains opportunity. Past earnings are included in my résumé enclosed.

Thank you! May I hear from you?

Cordially,

Jack P. Newton

Enc.

180

L. D. ERICKSON
180 Maple Avenue
Madison, WI 51612
Telephone: (608) 236-5050

Date

Mr. Jonathon R. Allison, President
Telemix Electronics Corporation
7418 Lehigh Avenue
Skokie, IL 60203

Do you, Mr. Allison, need in one of your plants a Manufacturing Manager? Engineering know-how has enabled me to handle Production management and liaison successfully, and my current objective is to continue to broaden my background in Manufacturing management.

If your present manufacturing volume, or its yield, could be materially increased by the introduction or further development of an engineered approach, you may be interested.

With 20 years of customer-oriented engineering experience in electronic equipment and products, I have:

As Quality Assurance Manager
—Achieved 100% correlation on short-and long-term warranty predictions over a 2-year projection.
—Provided engineering, technical, and analytical assistance in increasing customer acceptance levels by 33%.

As Quality Control Manager
—Reduced customer-use rejects 27% by product application liaison.

As Project Engineer
—Saved $40,000 a year in labor by analyzing a flow material application.
—Saved 6.9% total production process time through standards revision and process reduction.

This is the experience and the knowledge I can put to work for you. My résumé is available at your request. May I have a personal interview at your convenience?

Very truly yours,

L. D. Erickson

CARLTON F. MESSER
5612 South Alton Way
Englewood, CO 80112
Phone: (303) 771-5958

Date

Mr. Duane L. Fitzpatrick, General Manager
Burlingame Builders
1207 Market Street
Denver, CO 80201

Dear Mr. Fitzpatrick:

For the past five years I have been successfully handling construction
management in a very large general contracting business. I am now changing
positions, and I feel that your organization might need my services.

I know both construction management and construction engineering. Among my
accomplishments are these::

—With Atlas Construction Co. during the past five years, I've had personal
  direct charge at the job site for $50 million building construction.

—I know the techniques of maintaining construction *on schedule.*

—Years of contract administration success.

—I understand the value of cost control and the necessity for profit in
  building construction.

If you will let me talk with you for about 20 minutes, I believe I can assure you of
my value. I am available upon normal notice. My résumé is enclosed.

For your current or future need, may I come in?

Very truly yours,

Carl Messer

Enc.

WAYNE C. POWELL
248 Riverside Drive
Whitby, CN
Phone: (203) 818-7231

Date

Mr. Robert W. Peterson, President
Fashions, Inc.
412 Park Avenue
New York, NY 10026

Dear Mr. Peterson:

Time enough is still a problem, isn't it? Not scarcity of printout data, but time.

Perhaps you need more time to evaluate the conflict in information you already have. The conflict that you built in because you delegated profit responsibility to people, not to computers.

Has a Corporate, or Division President anything more important to do than taking the time for good decision making? Can some of the things he does, or wants to do, be handled by an Assistant having similar experience, maturity, and profit orientation?

This is what I can offer you to help build corporate profit:

—Comprehension of the essential elements in your business with the ability to establish, improve, or implement programs and procedures that contribute to corporate performance.

—Experience in saving substantial sums through operational and market analysis and the resulting improved management controls.

—Intelligence and skill in working harmoniously and productively with and through others at all levels.

My résumé is enclosed in great confidence, as my present company is not aware of my decision to consider a change.

May I talk to you?

Very truly yours,

Wayne C. Powell

Enc.

STANLEY L. KOLLMAN
2873 Hunter Road
Bennison, GA 30398
Phone: (404) 604-8743

Date

Mr. Matthew Rollins
National Marketing Manager
Invoco, Inc.
227 Peachtree
Atlanta, GA 30311

Dear Mr. Rollins:

Do your current or long-range plans call for a capable Manager of Market Research who has successfully demonstrated his ability to direct varied assignments and projects in the broad field of corporate planning and marketing?

With almost ten years of substantial experience in market research and its related fields, I can offer you:

    Personal involvement with leading projects in corporate planning studies, working with the highest levels of management in a $500 million international company.

    The ability to implement my professional work with productive and meaningful results that build sales and produce corporate profits.

I seek a new position of challenge, such as I visualize with your organization. Since my present employer is unaware of this decision to consider a change, my résumé is enclosed in the greatest confidence.

May I talk to you?

                 Very truly yours,

                 Stanley L. Kollman

Enc.

LOUIS J. WELTON
2411 Rosewood Lane
Bellevue, WA 98127
Phone: (206) 711-8812

Date

Mr. James Truax, Senior Vice President
Middleton Fund
48 Wall Street
New York, NY 10016

Dear Mr. Truax:

Will you take 30 seconds to read this letter? I'm looking for a new challenge to apply my substantial knowledge, and I'd like that challenge to be at Middleton Fund.

Fixed Income Portfolio Management is my area of competence. I am experienced in aggressive bond management for large pension funds, insurance companies, banks, and other sizeable portfolios.

As Fixed Income Portfolios Manager of a leading investment counsel firm in Seattle, I have full responsibility in an area of strong growth. I have demonstrated my ability to contribute materially both to my firm and to our clients.

I am willing to travel a reasonable amount and would relocate to New York if the potential were right. Earnings are negotiable above total current income. My résumé is enclosed in greatest confidence.

I'd welcome the opportunity to discuss how I might contribute as a part of your organization.

Very truly yours,

Louis J. Welton

Enc.

WILBUR N. DRAKE
3651 Thompson Terrace
Portland, OR 97213

Date

Mr. William Robard
Director of Executive Search
...
...
...

Dear Mr. Robard:

Successful Purchasing Management is my assignment in industry.

If profitability, excessive materials inventories, and increasing costs of manufacturing are now problems for a client company of yours, you may be interested in what I can contribute as Director of Purchasing or Materials Management. Some of my accomplishments are:

—Effected Departmental savings approaching $250,000 in one year for Nuclear Controls Corporation.

—Established a tight inventory control on 1,000 items for Motorola.

—Successfully set up a complete Purchasing Department, formulating all policies and procedures.

As an experienced Purchasing Director, I recognize the contribution Purchasing makes to corporate profit—often spending 50% of the sales dollar—and I know that a 2% savings in materials purchased may equal a 21% sales increase at a 5% profit level.

Current earnings are $46,000 plus options. I am willing to travel as required. My résumé is enclosed.

Your assistance in helping me relocate with one of your clients is appreciated. I'll be happy to talk with you at your request.

Very truly yours,

Wilbur N. Drake

Encl.

Phone: (503) 262–3913

MARTHA M. SENTILE
3612 Williston Boulevard
Minneapolis, MN 55431
Phone: (612) 724-2438

Date

Mr. Will Templeton
Templeton & Boxby, Inc.
...

...

Dear Mr. Templeton:

As an administrative generalist seeking a new affiliation, I offer your clients 20 years of corporate staff experience in marketing services administration and in office services management. I can bring to one of your clients who has a need for these attributes:

A dedication to the need for cost control to increase profits. The first page of my résumé illustrates this point.

A conviction that the best way to get the job done is by working effectively with people at all levels of the organization. I am comfortable with top management and know how to motivate my subordinates.

The ability to learn the essentials of new industries rapidly. Although I have had only two employers over the past 13 years, I have handled so many different assignments successfully that I now welcome the challenge of new situations.

Salary is negotiable in the general range of recent earnings. I am confident that I can do an excellent job for one of your clients. After looking over my résumé, I hope that you will give me a call. Thank you.

Sincerely,

Martha M. Sentile

Enc.

GIOVANI GENTINI
1503 Pleasant Hills Road
St. Louis, MO 63122
Phone: (314) 446-2506

Date

Director of Executive Search
...
...

Dear Sir or Madam:

Among your clients, there is a corporation that needs my ability to open new markets in the international field and to develop a strong sales or licensing organization.

I am in a position to help with the establishment of manufacturing facilities and markets where the investment and tax benefits will be advantageous to those U.S. companies that have not yet expanded overseas. During my two years residence in Belgium, I developed valuable contacts and relations, which will facilitate expansion of operations in Western Europe or which will enable a company seeking to enter that market to do so with minimum cost and maximum potential for success.

Due to my recent contacts with an Eastern Bloc country to promote diesel locomotives manufactured in that country, I feel particularly suited for handling export and licensing agreements of U.S.-made products in Eastern Europe.

Current earnings are $60,000 plus executive benefits. The aim of my present job search is to find a position in the aggressive market-opening field with a multinational corporation or with a company seeking to enter the international market. My résumé is enclosed in confidence.

May I hear from you?

Sincerely yours,

Giovani Gentini

Enc.

EDWARD E. TOMPKINS
Kelly, Malong & Tompkins
217 Broad Street
New York, NY 10004
Phone: (212) 932-1065

Date

Director of Management Services
...
...
...

Dear Sir or Madam:

Would a client company of yours have a need for a General Counsel to direct or handle all corporate legal affairs? I would appreciate your assistance as I make a job change from a law firm partnership to a corporate practice.

As you can see from the enclosed résumé, my years of top-level, broad experience have been in corporate law, including substantial success in trial work.

My current income is in excess of $75,000. My compensation could include a base salary, bonus, stock option, or other incentives. I know that you will treat the résumé in confidence.

Very truly yours,

Edward E. Tompkins

Enc.

HEINRICH G. THIESEN
2029 Hillside Avenue
Charlotte, NC 28209
Phone: (704) 372-9811

Date

Ms. Paula Jensen
Director, Executive Search Division
...
...
...

Dear Ms. Jensen:

It is my understanding that from time to time your clients call on you to provide management executives for them. May I tell you briefly about myself?

My field is Metallurgy, where I've held positions of increasing responsibility for the past eight years. At age 34, I'm now Manager of R & D after a promotion from Chief Metallurgist. I earn $41,000 a year plus benefits. I've been very successful in my work.

My prime motivation is to exercise my management as well as metallurgical abilities to the fullest extent. I want to handle Technical or Metallurgical Management at the corporate or divisional level. I know that you will treat the enclosed résumé in confidence.

Your assistance in helping me locate a similar position with one of your client companies would be much appreciated. I can arrange to be available to talk with you when you desire.

Thank you.

Very truly yours,

H. G. Thiesen

Enc.

RICHARD BETHANY
997 East Parkway Ave.
Columbus, OH 43221
Phone: (614) 273-0809

Date

Director, Executive Search
...
...
...

Dear Sir or Madam:

Somewhere in the U.S. or overseas, there may be a corporation that needs my
ability to turn things around, to trouble-shoot, to build profit, or reduce costs. I'm
a goal-oriented General Manager/Operations Manager who thrives on challenge
and needs to achieve. Currently, I've been running a $56 million Division with full
profit responsibility.

I am a Generalist, with a demonstrated record of building profitable sales and
reducing manufacturing costs through teams of people who get the jobs done.
Educated on the graduate level of engineering, I've handled general management,
manufacturing, purchasing, inventory control, marketing, and project and product
management.

The personal qualities I can offer are:

—Ability to identify the root cause of problems and organize a task force to
  solve them.
—Ability to learn new technology and new techniques, rapidly.
—Ability to stimulate others through ideas, energy, and purpose.
—Ability to develop and motivate people.

Do you have a client company that might need someone with my skills? I would
like to talk with you, and your assistance will be appreciated. Current earnings
are in the $65,000 range. My résumé is enclosed.

May I hear from you?

Very truly yours,

Richard Bethany

Enc.

191

WALTER H. ALLER
6721 West Allegherro Drive
Pittsburgh, PA 15238
Phone: (412) 437-0755

Date

Director of Management Services
...
...
...

Dear Sir or Madam:

For the past 19 years I've been successfully handling financial management assignments for Extron Steel Co. Principal functions have been in the Controllership area, with heavy emphasis on computer usage. My earnings are close to $50,000 a year plus benefits. A résumé is enclosed.

I seek a new opportunity to exercise my abilities to the fullest extent. While I know the steel industry thoroughly, it is not essential that I remain in this industry. My family is free to relocate. One preference might be the West or Southwest, but I'm willing to consider any location for the right potential. I am available now.

I will be grateful for your assistance in helping me to locate a similar position with one of your client companies. May I hear from you?

Thank you.

Very truly yours,

Walter H. Aller

Enc.

ROBERT B. BASCOMB
311 Evergeen Place
Barrington, IL 60010
Phone: (312) 381-2141

Date

Box 347-A
Wall Street Journal
711 West Monroe Street
Chicago, Illinois 60606

As you said in your November 23 ad in the *Wall Street Journal* for a National Retail
Sales Manager, your organization is in need of a capable sales/marketing
executive.

As my résumé outlines, I've had 8 years of solid national sales management
background. I'm experienced in sales administration and general marketing
management. I direct others effectively.

This is what I have done to help build corporate profit:

Directed point-of-purchase marketing tests that resulted in 100% increases
at full selling price.

Directed an all-media national advertising campaign that increased unit sales
by 30% and reduced advertising expenditures.

Initiated a new approach to home appliance merchandising in my territory,
which resulted in a 2% gross profit percentage increase.

In two years, I expanded sales in a hardware department catalog by $20
million with corresponding profit increases.

May I come and talk with you?

Very truly yours,

Robert B. Bascomb

Enc.

HARRIS L. JACKSON
317 Woodhaven Street
Courtney, NJ 07629
Phone: (201) 483-0054

Date

Bob MKB-2576
New York Times
229 West 43rd St.
New York, NY 10036

Your June 3 ad in the *New York Times* described your need for a Product
Development Manager. I am interested, for this could be the opportunity I seek.

My years of top-level experience with Borg-Warner and Bronton Industries, in a
wide range of engineering situations, may be valuable to you. This is what I can
offer you to improve results and reduce costs:

—The ability to relate applicable new developments to your Company's
problems and to grasp essential elements in need of attention.

—Experience in winnowing good ideas from bad and in balancing efforts
expended between current and new practices.

—Intelligence and the capacity to adapt prior experience.

—The faculty of working harmoniously with and through others on your
staff.

For specific achievements with the above companies, please see the résumé
enclosed.

May I talk with you?

Very truly yours,

Harris L. Jackson

Enc.

194

FRANK P. HUNTER
3498 Central Road
Birmingham, AL 35229
Phone: (205) 644-2212

Date

Ms. Helen McReady, Vice-President
First National Trust Company
390 Boca Raton Blvd.
Miami, Florida 33198

Dear Ms. McReady:

When I saw your Feb. 16 ad in the *Miami Herald* for an experienced trust officer, I knew at once that here was a position I could well fill. Thank you for making the requirements so clear.

Previous banking and trust experience, coupled with my abilities to work well with clients and associates, will let me contribute a good deal to the First National Trust Company.

In addition to the various accomplishments you see in my enclosed résumé, the following may be of interest:

Extensive trust business development. Tripled the trust volume for one small bank.

In another bank, opened 200 land trusts in five years; administered over 100 decedent's estates.

Elected to office in the Birmingham Bar Association.

I will phone you in a few days to see if we can set up a time for an interview, which can be arranged at your convenience. Should you wish to talk to me sooner, please call me at (205) 644-2212.

I look forward to seeing you.

Very truly yours,

Frank P. Hunter

Enc.

195

PAUL JOHNSON
1238 Greenfield Ave.
Cambridge, MA 02117
Phone: (617) 247-8162

Date

Ms. Nancy Paulino
Vice-President, Public Relations
McNeill Broadcasting
670 Boylston St.
Boston, MA 02107

Dear Nancy:

As you may know, I have made a decision to leave Multinational Chemicals, Inc. after about 10 years in Operations Planning and before that, 3 years in Research.

I plan to stay in my present field of Corporate Planning. I enjoy the challenge, and I have demonstrated my ability over a number of years. The results are there.

A copy of my résumé is enclosed, and I will be grateful for any thoughts you may have for me or any contacts you feel I should arrange to see.

Thanks, Nancy, I'll look forward to hearing from you.

Very truly yours,

Paul Johnson

Enc.

PAUL JOHNSON
1238 Greenfield Ave.
Cambridge, MA 02117
Phone: (617) 247-8162

Date

Ms. Nancy Paulino
Vice-President, Public Relations
McNeill Broadcasting
670 Boylston St.
Boston, MA 02107

Dear Nancy:

As you will recall, several weeks ago I gave you my résumé, after I had made the decision to leave.

This is just a note to say that I am now in the middle of an active job search; I am anxious to get established in a small or medium-size company as soon as possible. You know that I have demonstrated my ability, over several years, to take an assignment and wrap it up.

Another copy of my résumé is enclosed, and I will be grateful for any ideas you may have for me or any particular contacts you want to suggest.

Thanks, Nancy, I'll look forward to a call from you.

Very truly yours,

Paul Johnson

Enc.

11

Useful
Job-Search
Ideas

What are you doing when you are making a job search? You are marketing yourself, exactly like a manufacturer or a distributor or a publisher markets products. You, in this case, are the product. You need a marketing manager, and you know who that is. You will be using point-of-purchasing advertising—your interviews—as well as direct mail advertising—your broadcast and select employer mailings. If you realize what a job search is, you'll find it easier to carry out.

Your résumé is, as everyone acknowledges, your principal sales tool. It does not get you a job; it *could* get you to where the action is, the interview. You will want to use as many résumés as you can, in every situation in which a positive result is possible. The so-called shotgun approach of sending hundreds of form letters in hopes of a few responses is often costly and seldom productive; a mass mailing, each letter a rifle shot, is productive.

Another key ingredient in your job search is persistence. You must keep at it—answering ads, making phone calls, writing letters. Half-hearted or sporadic efforts only slow down your search. It's not easy to persevere when things aren't going well or according to your schedule, but you must keep moving. (It helps to have some much-needed support from family and a friend or two.) The momentum itself has value; it keeps your interest alive and doesn't let your natural enthusiasm die.

Working at your job search eight hours a day, seven days a week, is not feasible. You'll get tired too soon, no matter what you accomplish. Working full time at your job search should mean about five hours a day, five days a week, with perhaps a little extra time on Saturday. Weekend breaks are recommended therapy.

If you are currently employed, try for two hours a day and five hours on the weekend. That's an average of two hours a day, every day. To do that, plan to lock up the television and forget your usual evening newspaper and magazine reading.

If you've been dismissed as of a certain future date, see if you can arrange to stay on the payroll instead of taking a lump-sum severance pay. (This does not refer to pension-plan payments or other tax-related withdrawals.) Remaining on the payroll is both economically practical and psychologically beneficial. Find out, too, if your organization will permit you the use of an office, telephone, copy machine, and the services of a typist or secretary.

It should be common knowledge, but isn't, that the majority of the best jobs are never advertised. Why? Because employers get word-of-mouth recommendations from their contacts. This is true of a wide range of positions, from general managers of symphony orchestras, to key business positions, college teaching assignments, and association executive directors. What does this mean to you? That you must dig and dig for knowledge of openings. Don't forget how important your contacts are in this digging.

Information about potential employment opportunities could come from anyone, anytime, anyplace. At meetings and social gatherings determine whether it is appropriate to discuss your needs with one or two people present. Never make it a group discussion. Your efforts here should not be geared toward what these people themselves might do about hiring you as much as whom they may know who could help. Never even suggest that a contact could possibly hire you. If he or she is interested in you, you'll know soon enough. Other sources of information on potential employment opportunities are trade, business, and professional journals, as well as newspapers.

SUMMARY OF JOB-SEARCH PRINCIPLES

- Objective #1: to choose your job/career objective.
- Objective #2: to obtain interviews.
- Objective #3: to get the job that is right for you.
- An excellent résumé and well-written letters are essential tools. Most jobseekers use an average or poor résumé.
- Market yourself with a comprehensive plan. A well-planned campaign is a big advantage. Most people do not do this.
- Answer ads, write to employers, write to executive recruiters if appropriate, and use your business and personal contacts.
- Try to complete your search in a relatively short span of time. If possible, do not let the campaign stretch into five or six months.
- Maintain complete and accurate records of ad replies, letters written, telephone calls, and interviews. Keep copies of all letters and notes.
- Individualize all your efforts.
- Be well organized, confident, and persistent; do not procrastinate.
- At interviews, always maintain your best appearance. Do not be extreme in dress or personal grooming.
- If possible, keep your present employment until you get another job. It is best to conduct your full campaign while you are still actively employed.
- Handle yourself well in interviews. Practice first.
- Evaluate the offers carefully.
- Be prepared to spend enough time and money to do the job well. The cost is relatively small compared to the rewards of greater happiness and job satisfaction.
- It is more difficult to get a new job in another field or in another geographical location. So if you are going in that direction, you'll need to work even harder in your campaign.

DEVELOP A PROGRAM

A comprehensive position search/marketing plan consists of all or many of the following areas of activity:

- Letters to a selected few employers
- Want ads
- Executive search consultants
- Letters to many employers; mass mailings
- Business, professional, and personal contacts
- Trade and professional associations
- Other sources

Letters to Selected Employers

Don't confuse these comparatively few letters with employer mass mailings. These letters are individually typed (sometimes automatically typed if the quantity justifies), hand signed, and mailed using a commemorative stamp. Each employer is carefully selected after full research. Each letter is addressed to an individual who is in a position to hire you. Good research provides the list. These employers should be your prime sources because you have made the effort to select the organizations where you would like to work and those that might need you. You have, in effect, prescreened potential employers.

Alternatively, these selected employers might be the result of leads from one of your contacts. Such leads should be treated confidentially, acted upon promptly, and be given your best handling. If these leads don't produce a job offer, they may just produce more leads. You might get an employer name from want ads placed by that employer for other positions of no interest to you. You can decide whether or not to enclose a résumé. If it's good enough, your letter by itself might draw a response.

Want Ads

Want ads are a good source of job possibilities. They do tell you, about 95 percent of the time, that an unfilled position exists.

From a national or regional standpoint, major metropolitan newspapers have Sunday editions that normally carry the bulk of the display ads, such as the *New York Times*, the *Chicago Tribune*, the *Los Angeles Times*, and many others. The most important national paper for this purpose is the *Wall Street Journal*. Check the regional edition for your locality and the other *Wall Street Journal* editions if you want to or are willing to relocate. Normally, most ads appear on certain days of the week. Check the *Wall Street Journal* daily, not only to get the big-day pattern but to watch for key ads that appear on the off days.

If you do not live in or near a major city, check the nearest large city newspaper ads or the papers in the locality you are interested in. For your reference, here are principal newspapers located all over the United States, listed alphabetically by city. The list was prepared from data supplied by a public library. Your library will help you, too.

Akron Beacon Journal
44 East Exchange St.
Akron, OH 44328

Atlanta Journal-Constitution
72 Marietta St.
Atlanta, GA 30303

Baltimore Sun
501 No. Calvert
Baltimore, MD 21278

Birmingham News
P.O. Box 2552
Birmingham, AL 35202

Boston Globe
135 Morrissey Blvd.
Boston, MA 02107

Buffalo Courier Express
785 Main St.
Buffalo, NY 14240

Charlotte Observer
600 S. Tryon St.
Charlotte, NC 28232

Cincinnati Enquirer
617 Vine Street
Cincinnati, OH 45201

Cleveland Plain Dealer
1801 Superior Ave. N.E.
Cleveland, OH 44114

Columbus Dispatch
34 S. Third St.
Columbus, OH 43216

Dallas News
Communications Center
Dallas, TX 75265

Denver Post
P.O. Box 1709
Denver, CO 80201

Des Moines Register
Box 957
Des Moines, IA 50304

Detroit News
615 Lafayette Blvd.
Detroit, MI 48231

Houston Chronicle
800 Texas Ave.
Houston, TX 77002

Indianapolis Star
307 N. Pennsylvania Ave.
Indianapolis, IN 46204

Kansas City Star
1729 Grand
Kansas City, MO 64108

Louisville Courier-Journal
525 W. Broadway
Louisville, KY 40202

Miami Herald
1 Herald Plaza
Miami, FL 33101

Milwaukee Journal
333 W. State St.
Milwaukee, WI 53201

Minneapolis Star Tribune
425 Portland Ave.
Minneapolis, MN 55488

New Orleans Times-Picayune
3800 Howard Ave.
New Orleans, LA 70140

Oklahoma City Oklahoman
P.O. Box 25125
Oklahoma City, OK 73125

Omaha World-Herald
World-Herald Square
Omaha, NE 68102

Philadelphia Inquirer
400 North Broad Street
Philadelphia, PA 19101

Pittsburgh Press
P.O. Box 566
Pittsburgh, PA 15230

Portland Oregonian
1320 S.W. Broadway
Portland, OR 97201

St. Louis Post-Dispatch
900 No. Tucker St.
St. Louis, MO 63101

Salt Lake City Tribune
143 S. Main St.
Salt Lake City, Utah 84110

San Diego Union
P.O. Box 191
San Diego, CA 92112

San Francisco Examiner & Chronicle
110 Fifth St.
San Francisco, CA 94103

Seattle Times
Fairview, North & John
Seattle, WA 98111

Tampa Tribune
P.O. Box 191
Tampa, FL 33601

Washington Post
1150 15th St. N.W.
Washington, DC 20071

Stop and think about blind ads. An employer sometimes uses a newspaper or trade journal box number rather than disclose the organization's name and address. If you are unemployed or being terminated, go right ahead and answer blind ads. But if you are still employed and your search is confidential, be careful. The ad might have been inserted by your current employer.

If you want to relocate, subscribe to the leading newspaper in the city of your choice. Read it for a couple of months during your search. It will expose you to the display ads, as well as to the flavor of the community. It might produce unexpected ideas.

Executive Search Consultants

Any middle management, senior management, or executive job search should probably include executive search consultants, or executive recruiters as they are sometimes called. The likelihood of your getting a response from them isn't great, but the possibility does exist. One consultant, when queried, estimated that of all the searches made in one year, 5 percent or less of the executives placed were secured as a result of receiving unsolicited résumés.

Search firms are paid by employers, not applicants. Hence, their loyalty is first to a client firm or organization. Most recruiters will accept résumés mailed in by applicants. Many will not acknowledge a résumé, however, unless they have an interest in the jobseeker.

A few large firms, with numerous offices, have a business volume of many hundreds of thousands of dollars. Smaller offices, especially one- or two-person firms, will do much less as a result of fewer searches; your expectations should accordingly be lower. All firms operate with minimum salary requirements for the position to be filled. Some firms might have a salary minimum of $75,000 to $100,000; thus, they work primarily with top or senior executives, managers, or professionals. Smaller firms tend to have lower limits on position salary, some as low as $40,000 or less. Search firms usually consider $40,000 to $80,000 as a middle-management salary bracket.

What does a search firm do with a résumé they have no need for in their current assignments? Often, they toss it in the "round file." Other firms maintain extensive files for possible future requirements, saving those they want and discarding the rest. Should you send your résumé to a corporate outplacement firm? No. These firms are given jobseekers by their client companies, so they have no need for others.

What does an executive recruiter do with an applicant who does not have a good résumé but needs one? Nothing—which reiterates what has been said in the previous sections. Search firms need a complete résumé to work from. They want to know all about you, including birthdate, health, handicaps, marital status, children, willingness to relocate, and willingness to travel. They want to know who employs you now, for how long, and current position and salary. They need to know what your employer does. All of this requires full disclosure, preferably in your résumé, but at least in a cover letter.

Search firms tend to reject any résumé that doesn't fit current needs, omits full details about current employment, or tries to hide age, youth, terminations, or unemployment periods. Recruiters have a lot of experience and can seldom be fooled. Don't try.

Here are a few "rules" for dealing with executive search consultants:

- Send a résumé and a cover letter if you feel that you are an above-average professional or executive.
- Tell all about yourself, but concisely. Don't send three-to-four page letters; one page will do.
- Be honest.
- Don't walk into a recruiter's office without an appointment.
- Don't phone recruiters; write.
- Don't follow up by phone or letter.

Searches are conducted by executive search consultants, by search divisions of some management consultants, and by CPA firms. All operate in much the same way.

The Appendix tells you about the best source of information on search firms: the *Directory of Executive Recruiters*. This invaluable book may be at your public library. Use only the current annual edition for names and addresses. Buy a copy if you can't borrow one.

Letters to Employers: Mass Mailing

In contrast to letters to selected employers, individually tailored to each, the mass mailing or broadcast letter uses one well-written letter, produced by word processor or some form of automatic typewriter. For best results, each letter is addressed to the individual who has the authority to hire you. This is by far the best way to do it. Failing that, each letter can be addressed to a title, the holder of which would normally be able to hire you. Mass-mailing letters are sent out in quantities of 50, 100, or many hundreds. Hand sign all your letters.

Directories are your sources of employer names. In the Appendix, a representative list of directories is provided. If your field isn't listed, try the *Directory of Directories*.

For more localized potential employers, or smaller ones, check with the Chamber of Commerce for a membership list. See the local Yellow Pages. Printers often maintain and rent lists of employers in the community.

Broadcast letters are sent without a résumé. Your goal is to get a phone call to set up an appointment, or a letter requesting a résumé. Either way, the door is opened and you have a lead.

Business, Professional, and Personal Contacts

Some experts say that this is your single best source of job openings. They certainly may be right. Much depends on your relationship to these contacts and what you can persuade them to do for you. Most people seem to want to help their friends, although they may not always be able to do so. Contacts who want to help but don't may be too busy at work or plagued by personal problems. They may be immersed in some outside activity or just plain lazy. You must make an effort to secure their interest, then activate their help through regular reminders. These reminders should be made often enough to get them moving, but not so often as to pester them.

Hosting a lunch is a good way to go one-to-one with a

friend. Don't waste the hour explaining why you are changing jobs. Tell it in one or two short remarks and get on with your request for help. This isn't easy. Your friend might want to commiserate, and you might want sympathy. It is better to skip all this, however, because it won't help your job search. Give your guest a couple of résumés, explain your objective clearly, and say that you'll phone in a week if you haven't heard from him or her before then.

If you've built up many contacts in your career, you won't be able to take them all to lunch. Instead, use personal notes and enclose a résumé. Write a short, friendly note asking for help, making clear what you are seeking. Follow up with a phone call in five to seven days (your note might have landed in the big stack of "no rush" papers). Then, in another two weeks, send a follow-up note, along with another résumé. Perhaps you can arrange to run into this individual at a trade or professional meeting, a committee meeting, or at some community affair. Don't do anything but say "Hello." Seeing you is reminder enough.

Have you made a list of these contacts? Sometimes it is easier to prepare a three-by-five card for each one, showing name, work address and phone, home address and phone, and any pertinent data. Use the cards as your record of calls and notes you initiated, calls and notes you received, and other key information.

Your contacts may include professional associations, trade groups, and civic groups. Depending on how close you are to each, your list may include your lawyer, accountant, broker, and insurance agent. It probably should not encompass your neighbors and relatives; you might have many conversations with these individuals but little action. You cannot expect much from people who are only slightly acquainted with you; you probably shouldn't ask them.

Other Sources

These sources range from "less-than-likely to be productive" to "practically useless"; some are too costly for what you get. One reason they are discussed here is to alert you to some factors you may want to consider.

What about employment agencies? Without getting into the question of what separates a good agency from a poor one, the prime reason against using them is that they usually can't serve middle management executives, professionals, and senior executives. They do not handle assignments in the middle to upper dollar brackets. All the sources already discussed are more likely to be of help to you.

Should you place a position-wanted display ad in a newspaper? Probably not. It is costly and may create an adverse reaction in some employers. If you can afford it and feel sure you can reach the right readers, you could certainly try. You will get responses, but many will be from people who want to help you in your job search, for a fee.

In the *Wall Street Journal* and major metropolitan newspapers, you will see large display ads placed by firms known as Executive Guidance Counselors, Executive Career Counselors, or Outplacement Counselors. Investigate these firms if you wish, but don't do more than investigate until you feel comfortable about what they can do for you, and for how much. Be careful. Don't sign up on your first visit. You need to separate the competent and sincere from the incompetent, whose first concern is your wallet, not you. Some of these companies have very good salespeople. Some offer such a range of services that the fee you pay can be as much as $5,000 to $6,000. Do you really need career guidance, psychological testing, résumé preparation, job counseling, and interviewing assistance? There is no guarantee of the right position for you, or of any job, for that matter. Exercise great care. There can be value for you if you find the right firm and the right counselor. Perhaps a friend can recommend a particular organization.

FOLLOW THE PLAN

Now comes the hard part. You must follow the plan. All that work setting up your search methods is not an end in itself. It's only the means of making your search successful, with as little time-loss as possible.

It is a big mistake to decide you need a rest before starting your search. Perhaps you've been terminated with fairly good severance pay, so you won't run out of paychecks for a few months. Maybe you have concluded that some part of a pension-plan payment will be a lump sum in cash. So why not take a month off first, for a vacation or just to relax at home? Because it is a bad idea. You lose time, potential earnings, your drive to get established again, and some of the immediacy with your contacts. New employers won't react well when you try to explain what happened during the time when you were on "vacation." It pays to get going, certainly after a week or two at most.

Following your plan means doing what has to be done on schedule. Let the search plan become your way of life until you succeed.

MAINTAIN RECORDS

It is highly recommended to use three-by-five index cards for all segments of your search: one set of cards for contacts, one for selected employers, one for executive search consultants, and one set for want ads. Prepare a card when something develops the first time, then post that card as you go along. Prepare additional cards as needs arise. It is best to make a card for each of your contacts when you start your search. You might even prepare a full set of cards for the relatively few selected employers to whom you are writing. There is no need to make a full set in advance for your mass mailings.

Another way to maintain quick-glance records for want ads answered is to draw up a simple form like this:

Record of Position-Search Activity: Ads Answered

Organization, Location: Box No., Newspaper	Date of Ad, Position	Reply Date	Response Date	Follow-up Date	Interview Date

For employer activity, something like this will be useful:

Record of Position-Search Activity: Employers

Organization, Location: City, State, Zip, Phone	Individual & Title	First Letter	Résumé Sent	Follow-up Date	Interview Date

MAINTAIN POSITIVE ATTITUDE

There is no use pretending that your attitude is no problem at all. It's only natural sometimes to feel let down. But you'll be happier, healthier, and more effective if you can be positive in your approach. (You know that a good attitude is essential in interviews.) Two things can hinder you in your effort to maintain a good frame of mind: (1) a normal, human tendency to do only what seems essential at the moment, and (2) allowing discouragement to get to you. The best way to overcome these emotional "hang ups" is with your intellect. Reason tells you to proceed now, in spite of obstacles.

Good support from family and a loyal or trusted friend can mean a lot during your search. Don't elicit sympathy, however. Don't review how you lost your job, either in your mind or in talking with others. Self-pity and self-justification have no place in your positive attitude. Your future success is the matter at hand, not past failure or stroke of fate. You cannot waste time on these negative (but very human) influences.

USE THE TELEPHONE

The telephone is an instrument that can work wonders for you. It not only enables you to make the necessary outgoing calls to contacts and all others, it may also bring you what you've been waiting for; a call from an employer requesting a résumé or interview, or calls from contacts setting up new leads.

Outgoing calls merit little space in this handbook. You already know about friendliness, selling yourself, and asking the right questions. Make an interview date if you can, or arrange for another call. It's the incoming calls you might have to think about.

If possible, try to have an adult answer your phone when you aren't there. An employer or other key caller doesn't want his or her message misunderstood, garbled, or (especially with important items like call-back numbers) noted incorrectly, and neither do you. Perhaps young children could be instructed not to answer the phone. Teenagers could be instructed and trained in the serious matter of telephone technique for a job search. It can't hurt them to be willing to participate well in your job search.

One useful but expensive tool is an answering service. You can sign up with a service for a month or two on a full-time or part-time basis. You can also buy or rent an answering machine. In your absence, either of these methods of handling incoming calls is businesslike or professional, as the case may be. They cost money, but the value can be great. To find out more about answering machines, look in the Yellow Pages under "Telephone Automatic Answering Equipment." Do comparison shopping for costs and exact services expected, as these can vary greatly. Should you buy a machine or would renting one be better? Is the personal response of an answering service better for your purposes?

BE DISCREET

Tell only those you must about your job search, but no-body else. If an individual can't help you, don't tell him or her. This practice is good if you are unemployed or about to be. It's critical if you are working and your employer is unaware of your plans. If you are currently employed, there is always a certain amount of risk in a job search.

ESTABLISH REFERENCES

Individuals who will provide recommendations need to be seen or called in advance. They should be willing to give positive reports about you, and it is important for them to know what to say. This assumes that you know these people well enough to speak plainly to them. Each such person should know quite a bit about you personally and professionally, what your responsibilities were, what things you did exceptionally well, and where you worked. Each should be very familiar with your job objective and have a knowledge of how your achievements might benefit a new employer.

Alert each person who acts as your reference when you know that he or she might get a call.

BUILD YOUR CONTACTS

What if you have not built up a core of contacts thus far in your career? You can't do much about the past, but you *can* start to acquire contacts right now. Become a joiner in those areas where you have an interest, where you can genuinely contribute, and where joining can benefit you. Professional and trade associations are a good place to start. If you are unfamiliar with the various associations and their activities, consult the *Encyclopedia of Associations*, described in the Appendix, to see what is available in your field. Ask friends or others who may know.

Once you belong to an association, attend meetings regularly and plan to move up. Join one or two committees and then outshine everybody else. This isn't hard to do. Few people on a committee really give unstinted effort for a common cause where the return can't be measured except in satisfaction. Do your assignment just 10 percent better than others, and you'll be outstanding. Active committee work and its results can lead to membership on the board of directors, and then to the offices of the association. By that time, you'll have dozens of good contacts. You must give of yourself first, however; the benefits will accrue to you later. If this approach seems self-serving, rest assured that it is. Meanwhile, you will have contributed far more than most members.

Attend conventions, and if the scope is on the national level, your efforts for your local chapter can lead to higher assignments and to being on a first-name basis with national officials. Be of help to the executive director if you can. This is not textbook theory; this is exactly how it happens. Contribute, get the exposure, and don't burn any bridges.

You can give of your talents and time in many other areas as well. Serve well in your community. Local service clubs are pleased to have new and active members. What about alumni associations? What about some additional committees in church or other religious organizations? Don't forget that you give first, then receive.

TIME REQUIRED FOR A JOB SEARCH

The Executive Résumé Handbook can't tell how long your search will take, and neither can you or anybody else. It depends on how well you plan your search, how well you do it, the economic conditions in the country and in your field, what you have to offer, what appeals to the interviewer, and luck. What is luck? It is the hard work you do that other people do not do. Luck is being better prepared. Luck is handling an interview well, so that the chemistry takes a positive turn. Luck is making one more phone call, writing one more letter. Luck is studying this handbook, not skimming through it.

JOB-SEARCH CAPSULE IDEAS

- Make a good investment in yourself, in terms of both time and money.
- You don't have the job until you report for work; meanwhile keep all options open.
- Get the right job for you, not just any job.
- Focus on the present and the future; looking back can be devastating.
- Now is the time to search; don't wait for a "good time"; it will never arrive.
- High morale will help you; low morale will bring sorrow.
- Don't succumb to procrastination.
- Keep your records up to date.
- Make your phone calls when you should.
- Follow up all leads.

12

Interviewing for Corporate/Professional Positions

WHAT IS AN INTERVIEW?

There are many definitions of an interview and even more concepts of what it is. Be aware of what it shouldn't be when you are being interviewed. It is not an inquisition; it is not a speech by the employer on the merits of the organization; it is not a psychological test to see how you react to situations devised by the interviewer; and it is definitely not a device used by an opportunistic employer to buy you for less than you are worth to him or her.

Most people look upon an interview as a conversation in which each side gives and receives information. This is correct, as far as it goes. But for you, it is not only a communication in which information is exchanged, it is also a wonderful opportunity for you to make a friend. Friendship can often do as much for you in life as facts and logic. More friends can only help you, not hinder you, in your job search.

Be prepared for any kind of an interview and any kind of interviewer. While most interviews go along rather standard lines, some won't. An executive interview may be so well handled that you will hardly realize that you are being questioned or studied. Such an interview may seem to be just an ordinary conversation at first.

The usual format, however, includes: (1) an introduction by way of inconsequential comments, just to get acquainted; (2) some probing questions by the interviewer; (3) an opportunity for you to ask questions; and (4) a closing, at which time you should ask for the job (or not ask for it), while the interviewer will be doing a mental summing up to determine whether or not to consider you or see you again.

The interview coin has another side. The interviewer may do very little interviewing in the course of normal work. What little they do may be poorly done. What a spot to find yourself in! One solution, if you can carry it off, is to become the interviewer yourself and guide the discussion. Take charge! You can, if you are thoroughly prepared to present your abilities and achievements and explain how they can be applied to a new situation. As interviewer, it then becomes your job to bring out for the other individual the needs of the employer. You do the probing, and you supply the answers. When it becomes established that your presence on the job will aid the employer substantially, the time is right to let the interview flow into your need for challenge, opportunity, and reward.

There is no doubt that getting the interview is your first big hurdle. But once there, you are on your own to obtain what you seek. You can do it, too. Everyone has experienced personal interactions that have been successful. Have you ever gone to a retail store to buy clothes, and the salesperson, whom you have never met before, seems to understand what you want? The salesperson finds the right garment for you and a sale is made; you are a pleased and satisfied customer. This interaction was successful. What about when you meet someone socially for the first time, and he or she makes you feel comfortable? Sometime in the conversation a mutual interest arises. The encounter, lengthy or brief, goes well for both of you. Definitely a successful personal interaction. To make it happen you have to work at it. Be sincerely interested in the other person. Listen to what is said. Keep your mind wide open. Talk less yourself. You can work wonders. An interview is a highly important personal interaction. When you are offered the job, both you and the employer have gained what each of you wants.

Employers look for these things: (1) the right person (and personality) to fill the job as they see it; (2) someone

205

who can contribute over and above the demands of that particular job; (3) someone with executive and/or management experience and characteristics. As an applicant, you will be asking yourself these questions: (1) Do I want to work for this organization?; (2) Do I want this job?; (3) Can I fulfill the requirements?; (4) Will I fit in?; (5) Will this job and this employer give me work satisfaction and career progress?

SELLING YOURSELF

The interview is a splendid occasion to convey to an interviewer how you can contribute and why you should be selected over other applicants. Is this selling? It surely is. It takes skillful persuasion to get someone else to see things your way. That's selling! That's marketing yourself.

It is how you appear, how you act, and what you say that registers with an interviewer, as well as what the interviewer sees as your accomplishments, through his or her perspective. One key point in selling: keep the eye contact steady and your demeanor friendly. You are more likely to get hired if the interviewer feels that he or she likes you—not a very scientific fact, maybe, but a fact, nevertheless. Most interviewers will want to like you. Would they hire somebody who didn't appeal to them?

Selling isn't confined to just the person who interviews you, either. Selling includes everyone you come in contact with. The interviewer's secretary and other individuals in the reception room need to have favorable impressions of you. Their unseen votes can sometimes count for or against you.

Do you truly believe in yourself? You should. There is a right place for each individual, but yours may be hard to come by, unless you help. So help yourself first by knowing that you can do what you set out to do. Then, through marketing yourself and your talents, acquaint others with your efforts that have worked well for past employers. Selling, and in this case, selling yourself, is what brings a sound marketing plan to fruition. As long as you never hesitate to believe in your own value, selling yourself will never be a problem.

YOUR IMAGE STARTS WITH A FIRST IMPRESSION

Books and magazine articles have thoroughly covered the subject of grooming, conduct, and behavior at the interview. Even the subject of protocol (e.g., if offered, do you drink at a lunch meeting? Answer: no) has been written about. All of this is good in theory and makes for good reading. But now it becomes a very practical matter for you. Don't put off the needed trip to the hairdresser or the barber. Make sure that the appropriate clothes are available and clean. Do you have another outfit for a second interview? The vital point is that your wearing apparel must be right for the position and the organization. You won't go

wrong being conservative in your choice of clothes. Dress for the interview as you would expect to dress for the job.

Image isn't all clothing and hairstyle. Many other items make up the total picture of you. What about mannerisms? Small habits and actions become so much a part of you that you're not conscious of them. Do you keep your hand or finger on your chin or in front of your mouth? You speak less clearly if you do. Do you raise your eyebrows constantly? This becomes distracting. Throat clearing isn't terribly pleasant. Keys and glasses are necessary for their purpose but shouldn't be used as playthings in an interview.

If your normal custom is to slouch down in a chair, you are probably more comfortable in this position. You do not, however, present much of a picture of vitality and drive. Your new job might not call for drive, but your employer will certainly expect alertness.

Many, many interviewers are sharp people who know what to look for in an applicant. They notice the little things, without comment, and record them in their mental computers.

Try to avoid showing stress or anxiety. They make you frown and perspire and contribute negatively to the overall picture of a confident executive or professional. Stress is a natural, physiological reaction to a certain set of conditions. Being relaxed is the opposite. Granted, you have a great deal riding on an important face-to-face conversation. But if you keep your mind on how you could help the employer and how you are enjoying the opportunity to say so, you won't worry about failure. If this interview doesn't produce the magic words ("Mary/Bill, we'd like to have you join us!"), perhaps the next one will. Meanwhile, you've picked up some more interviewing experience and learned a thing or two.

One final suggestion about image and first impression: Just be yourself. Chances are that you will come across much better that way than if you try to be someone or something you aren't. If the first interviewer doesn't spot the make-believe, the second one might, at which point the game is over. Stretching the truth or pretending is hard work because you always have to remember what you said or did. It is hardly any trouble at all to be yourself.

MAKE THE MOST OF YOUR INTERVIEW

If you have succeeded in obtaining an interview, you have acquired a time and place to create a favorable image, to sell yourself, to tell of your experience, and to demonstrate how your achievements can be put to better use—all of which may solve an employer's problem. He or she has one or more problems for sure, or you wouldn't be sitting there.

Some people will consider this next thought to be naive, but it could be important in the long run, as well as in the short run: You have an opportunity to make a new friend—someone who may not necessarily hire you, but who could give you another lead, or another contact. Individuals seldom go out of their way for people they don't care about. Friends help friends.

If you've done your homework, you've learned a great deal about the organization, but you know little about the position that's open or about your potential superior-to-be. So another basic is to get some vital data not previously available. Decide before the interview what you need to know to enable you to evaluate the position intelligently.

You are in this interview to do what your résumé and letters could not do. In a face-to-face discussion you can explain how you accomplished the highlights you brought out in your résumé. You can also explain how the methods that brought about your past results can be applied to the new problems you did not even learn about until this interview.

You are here to get the job. This is your immediate goal, and there is no other, or better, place or time than right here, right now!

PREPARING TO BE INTERVIEWED

Plan each interview. The interviewer does. You should, too. Know all you can about the potential employer. The Appendix lists directories that contain a wealth of information. Prepare your own set of questions and work them into the give-and-take of the interview exchange. Prepare your answers to the possible questions an interviewer might ask you. See if you can locate someone who has worked for the employer, and find out about the organization, your boss-to-be, and the job itself.

Your preparation should begin early, because last-minute crash efforts seldom work out well. Some preparatory steps are general in nature, while others are down-to-earth ideas to use just prior to and during each interview. Here are thirteen preparation suggestions, applicable to almost any interview you will have:

- Study your résumé. Review what you have to sell and how best to sell it.
- Plan to be yourself.
- Be well rested, physically and emotionally.
- Practice interviewing. Learn to answer, not wander. Learn to be brief. Line up some interviews for jobs you don't want—just for the practice.
- Know who you'll see, at an exact time and specific location.
- Make sure that your grooming and dress are correct.
- Be on time, which means five to ten minutes early. Tardiness is inexcusable, so allow for a traffic accident tie-up, a train crossing your highway, a hard-to-find parking lot, or a two-block walk to the building entrance.
- Don't get agitated if you are kept waiting; usually the interviewer can't help it.

- Be mentally prepared to adopt a good attitude, and be responsive.
- Let your employer talk at the beginning of the interview, while you listen.
- When you speak, dwell on your successes, not your responsibilities. These are two different things.
- Remember your goals in the interview.
- Avoid planning interviews too close together.

SPECIFIC GUIDANCE

Here are twenty-nine common-sense suggestions and points of behavior, under the headings of "Listening," "Speaking," "Alertness," and "Actions." These recommendations are useful guides during an interview itself. No one item on this list is crucial by itself, but together they add up. You already know these twenty-nine suggestions or have read similar ones in other sources. Study them anyway, as a refresher. You want to handle an interview right the first time; there is no second chance.

LISTENING

- Listen well. Be truly interested in the interviewer as a person.
- Do not interrupt; your turn will come.
- Listen for positive remarks that show you are being well received.
- Listen for a job offer.

SPEAKING

- Speak well; clearly, not too fast, with a freshness in your voice. Keep eye contact. Use correct grammar. Say what you have to say, then stop.
- When speaking of past employers or bosses, be honest, give short answers, do not downgrade, and get off the subject.
- Ask a question when silence prevails.
- Have examples of your achievements on tap.
- Avoid discussing your own strong biases, and steer clear of religion and politics.
- Never argue; if you win, you lose.

ALERTNESS

- Watch for the hidden opportunity—the other job the interviewer knows about that you don't.
- You are interviewing the interviewer, too.
- Conduct yourself according to the tone of the interview.
- Forget about anyone you already know in the organization.
- Your personal problems are your own; don't discuss them.
- Keep your temper in check; it could be costly.
- Should the interviewer get an outside interruption, plan your next strategy.

- The interviewer decides when the interview is over, you don't.

ACTIONS

- Practice courtesy and use good manners.
- Be friendly, conservative, and quietly enthusiastic.
- Smile easily.
- Do not smoke.
- Avoid unusual approaches or gimmicks.
- Keep your ego submerged. Never show up an interviewer.
- Skip the drinks at a luncheon interview.
- When the interview is over, stop talking and prepare to leave.
- Find out what happens next.
- Shake hands firmly.
- Don't use hard sell; it doesn't work.

WHAT INTERVIEWERS ASK

What interviewers ask in an interview may depend on whether the policy of the organization is to use a patterned interview, with set questions, or an informal one-on-one meeting. The former style can keep the interviewer on course but could get to be a ritual; the latter could lead to aimless wandering with badly orchestrated questions that contribute little to the final decision.

Both applicants and interviewers can be guilty of bluffing or of covering up deficiencies. Still, the long-established place of an interview in the employment process is set in concrete and will no doubt continue to be a keystone to getting hired. So it makes sense for you to understand the process, from the points of view of both sides of the table. Since there are many kinds of interviewers, there will be many kinds of questions.

Employers have to start somewhere, so they often ask what may seem to be odd questions. (This is less likely to be the case in professional and management circles than at lower levels.) You should respond with friendly, serious-minded answers and wait until the essentials begin to show up. Consider these typical questions:

- "Who are you, really?"
- "Well, what shall we talk about?"
- "Why do you want to work for us?"
- "What do you think you can do for us?"
- "Are you employed now?" "Why not?"
- "Why did you leave your current job?"
- "Do they know you are leaving?"
- "Tell me about your education."
- "Tell me about your work history."
- "What are your salary needs?"

Do you notice how these introductory questions could prove upsetting, if you aren't prepared? Many of the questions are invitations for long, rambling statements on your part. Resist the temptation to reply at length. Give brief answers, and ask a question yourself. If you told an interviewer everything about your education, you could use up half the interview time to no avail. Limit yourself to the pertinent facts. Under no circumstances should you answer directly anything about your need for a certain level of pay. If it develops that an organization wants you, it will meet any reasonable salary requirements.

Capable and competent interviewers ask pertinent questions. If you are fortunate, you'll run into these individuals. In each case, make the most of it by discussing, person-to-person, how your presence could be beneficial to this employer.

One more word of caution. Do not let questions about extracurricular activities get you into an enthusiastic, long-winded tale of your favorite sport or how you got elected to the school board. Be especially careful about the evening classes you have taken and have done well in. If they are relevant, mention them. If not, don't waste time. One danger area might be too many self-improvement courses, which could be interpreted as a lack of confidence on your part.

WHAT YOU CAN ASK

When the usual polite preliminaries are over, try to get into the current situation and the job-opening as quickly and smoothly as you can. The interviewer may assure you that there is plenty of time, but you know, and he or she knows, that there isn't all that much time.

You will have prepared some key questions in advance. See how the following queries lead right to where you want to be—that is, what the problem is and how you can be of help in solving it.

- "Would you tell me about this position?"
- "Whom would I report to?"
- "What are the current problems where my experience could help produce the solution?"
- "What's been done so far?"
- "Which problem is most urgent?"
- "What is the deadline to get this straightened out?"

Follow such questions with normal inquiries about the organization, its goals and plans. Show how your experience/achievements can fit this bill. You will finally get to the matter of being hired, and at what salary. Ask about benefits last, although today they are a substantial part of the total compensation package.

Do not ask the probing questions you have prepared until the little questions are answered. Early in a get-together is not the time to upset the interviewer with questions that he or she will probably feel comfortable answering after some community of interest is established.

It's similar to a social situation. In due time, your interviewer might be inclined to share personal thoughts with you. Special questions might include:

- "Why is the position open?"
- "How long has the position been vacant?"
- "Did the individual who had the job get promoted?"
- "Will you tell me something about the person to whom I would report?"

HOW YOU CAN HELP DURING THE INTERVIEW

As an executive, you realize the level of the position for which you are interviewing, and you conduct yourself accordingly. You understand corporate/professional protocol. You are courteous. But there is one other important factor. You should consider yourself on an equal footing with the interviewer. You aren't begging for a job; you are offering an employer an opportunity to hire you so the problems can be solved and the job can be handled successfully.

Thus, your attitude is professional. You can discuss with the employer what the job is, its level, its difficulties. You can swing the conversation into "how we can handle this problem."

You can help by keeping the interview on track. Cut off the tangents quietly but as firmly as you can without being pushy. In some cases, you can gain control of the interview, but be very careful with it. You want a grateful interviewer, not a resentful one.

Keep uppermost in your mind the fact that the employer is thinking about what he or she wants, not what you want. So in business situations talk about sales increase, profit development, greater market share, cost cutting, advertising results, or whatever problem you've discovered. In other fields, talk about whatever is the main thrust: grants, budgets, community acceptance, membership increase, curriculum development, and so on.

HELP THE LESS-EXPERIENCED INTERVIEWER

If an interviewer is relatively inexperienced, help out. Keep the conversation going. Be sincerely understanding of the predicament. You can make a friend, and a friend is what you need at this point. Helping the interviewer helps you.

Show by your attitude and your grasp that you can expect positive results from an interview. You'll probably get a positive response.

THE INTERVIEW PORTFOLIO

Should you prepare a portfolio? And if you do, should it go with you on the first interview or be saved for future meetings? Your answer to the first question depends on your personality and your ability to present a clear picture without the use of props. Put another way, if you feel that a high-quality portfolio will be of any assistance, then prepare it. Like all your other steps, quality counts.

A portfolio might not prove to be necessary on the first interview, but if you need it and don't have it, one sales opportunity has been lost. How about making the portfolio to fit inside your attaché case? Keep it in the case until you need it.

Many people tend to build portfolios that are too large. This is not an ego exercise. Omit everything that is not a definite plus toward your job-search goal. You quickly lose an interviewer if you force attention on irrelevant areas—irrelevant, that is, in the employer's mind. A portfolio enables you to communicate visually with the interviewer. It is your collection of data and material to show your competence in prior positions.

To assemble one, prepare a three-ring or similar binder, probably using plastic protective sheets. Your achievements can be indexed and filed by functional areas of experience for ready reference. Include a copy of your résumé. Include sales and profit charts, letters that produced results, procedures that were successful, financial forms designed, marketing plans that were effective, or research that brought results. Include pictures of products, stories of customer or plan problems solved, or list of patents. In professional areas, include effective examples of your work. In addition, outside activity references may be useful but should be used sparingly. Include copies of articles and lists of publications. In all work areas, include talks given and important press clippings.

Use the portfolio carefully and sparingly in an interview. Use it only to illustrate a point or a problem you solved, then close it and put it away. Do not let the interviewer read the entire kit at once. You must physically control the portfolio at all times.

AFTER THE INTERVIEW IS OVER

Immediately after the interview and outside the interview building, jot down all the pertinent areas covered. How was it concluded? Who is to call whom? When? Is anything to be mailed tonight? These are vital items, and your notes must be clear to avoid any slip-ups. Do what you must, on time.

Next, record areas stressed by the employer. What were the problems you might be required to solve? What was said that was positive for you as an applicant? Are there any negatives to be overcome in your "thank you" note?

Write down all the names mentioned, even casually, along with position and level. Whom will you report to and work with? Record your own reactions to the interviewer. To what things did he or she respond favorably?

Your "thank you" note should be brief, friendly, and indicate your expectation of another talk. Include one or two experience highlights, not previously used, that you believe will strike a receptive chord. Write the note within twenty-four hours of the interview, and write it regardless of what the outcome was or what you anticipate it will be. Let this letter be one more soft-sell sales effort on your part. And remember, you were going to attempt to make a new friend. The interviewer-friend may prove to be extremely helpful in some unexpected way.

Mark your ever-faithful calendar pad for any follow-up call you are scheduled to make or that you want to make anyway. Would calls to anyone else be useful? Should you call your references to alert them of possible letters or telephone calls?

Reflect upon whether or not you want this job if it were offered or if you expect it might be. You might want to look back to chapter 3 and consider the items you listed in your job-change chart.

After the conclusion of the interview, review what happened. Try to think of what went well and what did not. If you made any mistakes, determine to correct them. Were there any areas you know that you could improve upon next time?

THE JOB OFFER

After a few weeks, or many months, of searching, the great day arrives when you get a job offer. What should you do? The basic rule is this: If you are almost starving, desperate for money, and it has been a long, arduous struggle, take the job then and there. But if not, be receptive and eager but ask for a short time to consider it. Almost every employer who does make you an offer actually wants you because you appear to be the best bet for the opening. If he or she didn't think this, no offer would have been made. What a "short time" is depends on a lot of things, but the higher the job level the longer you probably have to decide. One or two weeks is about the minimum amount of time for professional, management, or executive positions, in the lower brackets. Ask the employer if the time you have suggested is reasonable. Be prepared to reduce it if you have to. This "thinking it over" time allows you a breather and prevents you from making a premature leap in the wrong direction. While an employer may have taken a long time to make the offer, once it is made he or she expects action. Be guided accordingly!

Do not expect an employment contract unless you are in the higher brackets. A letter of agreement will sometimes be given. It spells out the details of the job that has been proffered: Starting date, salary and benefits, and first review date may be included. But it doesn't bind the employer to anything other than what the letter says. It won't be written to protect you but to protect the employer. If you were the employer, you would no doubt write it the same way.

Take heart. No matter what job you accept, if you are a good executive, do your job well, and produce results, you can expect a reasonably long tenure in the position. Meanwhile you are expanding your horizons, creating new achievements, and moving along your career highway.

13

Achieving Success

The Executive Résumé Handbook has endeavored to convince you that you have assets to offer an employer for his or her benefit as well as your own, that quality pays off, and that if you work at it, your job search will be successful. You set your job goal, and you know that it can be reached.

The tools you create can be better than those most job-seekers have. Your executive or professional résumé and your good and full use of business, trade, and personal contacts are indispensable means to a most desirable end. You are not seeking just a job but the job of your choice.

This handbook has tried to give you the mechanics of a good job search. It has also tried to give you more; the techniques are important, but they are not the job. In the final analysis they are only the paraphernalia of a job search. The real crux of the matter is you, what you do, and how you do it.

Many executives are so eager to move into action quickly that they do not plan well, if they plan at all. The job-search ideas in *The Executive Résumé Handbook* have given you a good overview of how to go about making a comprehensive plan. You know that you have to keep on working hard at your plan, just as you would do in your usual work position. You must take care of high-priority items first, then turn to less urgent things.

Where do you really win or lose? At the interview with the person who has the desire and the power to hire you! As chapter 12 pointed out, a successful interview is an achievement for both applicant and employer. Just remember to be you, and try to establish a good rapport with the interviewer. If you have planned well and are working harder at your job search than most other applicants, you will ultimately get the job. Some people quit after a couple of efforts, some will try for a goal five times and then give up. You keep trying after you've heard "no" ten times, or maybe fifteen. Employer number sixteen may be ready to say "yes" to *you*.

Yesterday is gone; tomorrow is still ahead and can be exciting and rewarding. Today is what you have to work with. Today is the time of great opportunity. Take advantage of it.

APPENDIX

Before beginning any research with directories, get acquainted with the reference librarian at your local public library. You'll be glad you did. The help you can receive is invaluable with respect to both knowledge and time. In addition, librarians are known to have an innate desire to assist their patrons. Make use of this rare attitude.

DIRECTORIES: BUSINESS, INDUSTRIAL, FINANCIAL

Directory of Corporate Affiliations. National Register Publishing Co., Wilmette, IL. Annual.

Lists 4,000 U.S. parent companies, with their divisions, subsidiaries, affiliates. Geographical index by state and city. SIC index.

Dun & Bradstreet's Million Dollar Directory. New York. 5 volumes. Annual.

Vols. 1, 2, 3: Alphabetical list of companies with a net worth of $500,000 or more; Vol. 4: the top 50,000 concerns, those with a net worth exceeding $1,850,000; Vol. 5: A cross-referenced index.

Includes 160,000 industrial companies, banks, utilities, wholesalers, retailers, and others, with address, principal products, sales, employees, SIC (Standard Industrial Classification) numbers, officers, and directors.

Dun & Bradstreet's Reference Book of Corporate Managements. New York. Annual. 4 volumes.

Professional histories of tens of thousands of principal officers and directors of more than 12,000 U.S. companies. Cross-referenced by geography and industry.

Encyclopedia of Associations. Gale Research Co. Detroit. 3 volumes. Biennial.

Vol. 1: 20,000 national associations in the U.S. Detailed descriptions of trade, business, commercial, professional, and other organizations arranged by seventeen subject categories; Vol. 2: Geographic/executive index, covering material in Vol. 1; Vol. 3: Listings of new associations and projects (not an update).

Encyclopedia of Business Information Sources. Gale Research Co. Detroit.

Lists of sixteen kinds of sources on more than 2,000 topics; arranged in alphabetical order.

Forbes Magazine. New York. Semimonthly.

Special Spring issue: annual directory of 500 largest U.S. corporations; sales, profits, assets, market value. Chief executives of companies, with addresses; January, first issue: covers seventeen industries, ranking companies by profitability and growth.

Fortune Magazine. New York. Monthly.

May issue: 500 largest U.S. industrial corporations; June issue: 500 second largest corporations; July issue: largest nonindustrials: banking, insurance, financial, retailing, transportation, utilities.

MacRae's Industrial Directory. MacRae's Blue Books Co. New York. 5 volumes. Annual.

Vol. 1: An alphabetical corporation index that provides addresses, offices, capital ratings, products or services, and a trade-name index; Vols. 2–5: a product classifications index, organized alphabetically.

Martindale-Hubbell Law Directory. Martindale-Hubbell, Inc. Summit, NJ. 7 volumes. Annual.

Lists by states and provinces the Bar of the U.S. and Canada plus foreign countries. Complete information on lawyers and law firms.

Moody's Manuals. Moody's Investors Service. New York. Annual.

Six of the manuals are of particular interest: Bank and Finance, Industrial, OTC Industrial, International, Public Utility, Transportation. Comprehensive information about each company, including corporation history, subsidiaries, plants, products, officers.

Polk's World Bank Directory. North American Edition. R. L. Polk. Nashville, TN. Semiannual.

Geographic lists of banks, with officers and directors, assets and liabilities, branches.

Rand McNally International Bankers Directory. Chicago. 4 parts. Revised on a semiannual basis.

Geographic lists of U.S. and large foreign banks. Alphabetical index. Data similar to *Polk's World Bank Directory* (above).

Standard Corporation Records. Standard and Poor's Corporation. New York. 7 volumes. Annual.

Material similar to *Moody's Manuals* (above).

Standard Directory of Advertisers. National Register Publishing Company. Wilmette, IL. Annual.

Classified Edition: 17,000 companies advertising on a national basis, listed by fifty-one product classifications; includes sales, employees, officers, advertising agencies. List of one hundred top advertisers plus leading agencies; Geographical Edition: advertisers arranged by state and city.

Standard and Poor's Register of Corporations, Directors and Executives. New York. 3 volumes. Annual.

Vol. 1: 45,000 U.S. and Canadian companies, with officers, products, SIC, sales, and employees; Vol. 2: 72,000 executives and directors, listed alphabetically; Vol. 3: Index of companies by SIC number, geographic location, corporate family

State Industrial Directories.

Issued for the various states, listing manufacturers alphabetically, geographically, and by SIC. Usually provides complete data on each entry.

Thomas Register of American Manufacturers. Thomas Publishing Company. New York. 19 volumes. Annual.

Part 1: 120,000 manufacturers by specific product or service; Part 2: Alphabetical list with addresses, subsidiaries, asset classification; Part 3: Company catalogs, alphabetically bound.

Who's Who in Finance and Industry. Marquis Who's Who. Chicago. Biennial.

Short career data on leading business people in finance and industry, with specifics of position, vital statistics, writings, address.

One book deserves special mention because it may help solve some reference problems if the directories listed above do not meet your individual needs:

Directory of Directories. Gale Research Company. Detroit.

This guide to business and industrial directories, professional directories, and others provides reference data on about 8,000 directories of various types. Sixteen classifications. Title index and subject index, with cross-references.

EXECUTIVE SEARCH, MANAGEMENT CONSULTING, AND CPA CONSULTING FIRMS

If you plan to send your résumé to executive search firms, there is an ideal directory containing a gold mine of information:

Directory of Executive Recruiters. Consultant News, Templeton Road, Fitzwilliam, NH 03447. Tel.: (603) 585–2200.

The main section lists alphabetically the Retainer Recruiting Firms, which operate on an advance retainer basis. These are the "purists" of the executive search field. They are paid by an employer client, whether or not a search is successful. This group includes executive search consultants, management consultants with executive search divisions, and several CPA firms with executive search divisions.

The second part of the main section lists the Contingency Recruiters—agencies and other executive recruiting firms that work on a fee-paid basis payable on placement. They are paid by employer clients if a search is successful.

The directory lists 2,000 firms and offices. It contains a cross-index by functions, such as general management, manufacturing, or administration, for a total of about eighty-five. There is also a cross-index by industries, a geographical cross-index, and a list of key principals of the firms. Your local library may have a copy. If it does not, or has only an out-of-date edition, order your copy from the publisher. Issued annually, the price is under $25, and worth it.

INDEX

ABOUT THE AUTHOR

HAROLD W. DICKHUT is president of Management Counselors, Inc., a consulting firm that he has headed for more than fifteen years. Previously, he served as general manager of Stivers Temporary Personnel, Inc., a national temporary help service, and was executive vice-president of Automation Institute, a Chicago business school. His professional teaching experience includes posts at Metropolitan School of Business in Chicago, North Park College, Roosevelt University, and Northwestern University. He is the author of *The Professional Resume & Job Search Guide* (New York: Prentice Hall Press, 1981).